'Few people get to the heart of an audience as sensitively and as deeply as Rob Parsons.'

Dr John Gallacher, Professor of Cognitive Health, University of Oxford

'Rob Parsons is one of the most inspirational speakers in the country today – motivating, practical, and giving you the sense that somebody has just turned a light on.'

Rosemary Conley, author and broadcaster

'Rob has an uncanny ability for asking some of life's most challenging questions in an unobtrusive way.'

Jill Garret, former Managing Director, The Gallup Organisation, UK

'I was once told: "If you want to improve your golf, play with someone far better than you and watch them carefully." The same is true of many things in life. Rob Parsons is in the Premier Division of communication skills, and in this book, he shares insights and advice honed through experience. Read it and apply the lessons – your listeners will be glad that you did.'

Ian Coffey, Vice Principal (Strategy) and Director of Leadership Training, Moorlands College

'We asked Rob to come and inspire, challenge and motivate our conference of three hundred partners, directors and managers. He certainly did this and more . . . so much so that we've booked him again!'

Tim Richardson, Development Leader,
Financial Services Division, PwC Global

'I have dedicated my life to preaching and writing – including twenty-five years at Westminster Chapel – and yet I believe there is so much to learn from this remarkable book.'

Dr R.T. Kendall, author of Total Forgiveness

'Rob Parsons was a first-rate speaker, with the ability to get his audience to ask themselves some fairly hard questions without spoon-feeding or antagonising them.'

'I wish I had heard that lecture ten years ago.'

'The subject matter was very thought-provoking and the delivery little short of an art form!'

From a KPMG leadership lecture

'Over a long career in international business, I have heard many motivational speakers. Rob Parsons is one of the finest . . . not only in his presentation skills, but in the importance of his message, which is vital for British industry.'

*George Russell, former Chief Executive of
Scotland the Brand, former head of Food
& Agribusiness at Scottish Enterprise*

'A superb, thought-provoking address.'

'I'll never forget what you said and I'll be putting it into practice.'

The Royal College of Surgeons

'Rob Parsons is quite simply one of the UK's very best communicators. He has spent more than fifty years developing his unique gift. I know we all have so much to learn from him.'

Andy Hawthorn, OBE, founder of The Message Trust

The Heart of Communication

• • •

*How to really connect
with an audience*

Rob Parsons

HODDER &
STOUGHTON

First published in Great Britain in 2020 by Hodder & Stoughton
An Hachette UK company

1

Copyright © Rob Parsons, 2020

The right of Rob Parsons to be identified as the Author
of the Work has been asserted by him in accordance with
the Copyright, Designs and Patents Act 1988.

A CIP catalogue record for this title is available from the British Library

Hardback ISBN 978 1 529 37341 7
eBook ISBN 978 1 529 37343 1

Typeset in Adobe Garamond by Hewer Text UK Ltd, Edinburgh
Printed and bound in Great Britain by Clays Ltd, Elcograf S.p.A.

Hodder & Stoughton policy is to use papers that are natural, renewable
and recyclable products and made from wood grown in sustainable
forests. The logging and manufacturing processes are expected to
conform to the environmental regulations of the country of origin.

Hodder & Stoughton Ltd
Carmelite House
50 Victoria Embankment
London EC4Y 0DZ

www.hodder.co.uk

To John Loosemore – thank you for the inspiration, the support and the laughs.

And to Lyndon Bowring – for sitting at the back with your notebook. You made me a more effective speaker.

Contents

• • •

Acknowledgements

• • •

As ever, I am grateful to a whole team of people including Katharine Hill, Paula and Tom Pridham, Robin Vincent, Paul Francis, Gerrit Bantjes, Kate Hancock, Stephen Hayes, Esther Holt, and the team at Care for the Family.

Special thanks to the brilliant Sheron Rice – once again you made my book better! I am grateful to work with the team at Hodder and Stoughton, especially Ian Metcalfe and Andy Lyon. My agent Eddie Bell of the Bell Lomax agency offered encouragement, advice and sheer wisdom – thank you.

And finally, thank you to my wife Dianne – for everything.

CHAPTER 1

Find One Thing That Can Make a Difference

• • •

I believe I can help you be a more effective public speaker.

I say this because, for over half a century, I have not only listened to some of the best (and, no doubt, a few of the worst!) public speakers in the world, but I have *watched* them. And if I had to single out one characteristic of those who are the most effective communicators – whether they are addressing audiences of thousands or speaking to seminars of twelve – it would be this: they are teachable. They are tireless in their effort to 'stir up the gift within them'. They want to get better.

I have long given up taking part in arguments as to whether those who become the most successful in a particular field – whether it's sport, music or business

– do so because they are more gifted than others or because they are more committed. But I am sure of this: the world is full of people who have an incredible natural gift but never reach their potential because they believe they have nothing left to learn and stop trying to develop that gift. On the other hand, there are those who achieve far above what was predicted for them because they simply work hard to get better in their chosen field. And when you see somebody at the very top of their profession – whether they are a football player, a violinist, Formula One driver or a teacher – they have two qualities: natural gift and an incredible dedication to improve. Sir Alex Ferguson was so convinced of this that having watched and trained some of the most gifted footballers in the world, he said, 'Hard work will always overcome natural talent when talent does not work hard enough.'

Some years ago, I attended a conference of five thousand people. As well as main-platform talks in the huge auditorium, many smaller seminars were taking place, and I noticed one entitled 'Developing your public speaking'. When I told a colleague that I intended to attend it, he said, 'Why bother? You're speaking tonight to four thousand people!' I replied, 'Trust me, it'll be worth it.'

When I arrived, there were a hundred or so delegates there, but, so far as I could see, none of the other conference speakers. To be honest, I'd heard most of what the speaker said before, but I have always been prepared to read a book or listen to a talk for just one good idea and on this occasion I was not disappointed. About halfway through his presentation, he said two things that impacted my public speaking from that day on. I'll tell you the first now, and I'll come back to the second later in the book. He said, 'When you address an audience you will lose their attention for one of two reasons: because you're boring or because you're interesting.' I remember thinking, 'How on earth would you lose somebody's attention because you're interesting?' He explained, 'You'll say something that will really grab their attention – so much so that they'll start to think about it, their minds going off in a different direction. If you want to keep the audience with you for the whole of your talk, every so often you must do something to bring them back. It may be by changing your pace or the pitch of your voice, introducing a story or simply taking your jacket off. But if you are going to keep them for the whole of your talk – you've got to get them back.'

I know the first line of this book sounds presumptuous – after all, some of you may be among the most effective communicators in the world. But since you are reading this book, you are probably, like me, searching for that one idea that can make a small difference. I pray you find it.

When I was about sixteen an older man from our church, Arthur Tovey, said to me, 'I think God has given you a gift of public speaking – and I'm going to teach you.' I remember thinking at the time that there were at least two problems with that. First, I didn't take part in debates or drama at school – I didn't even put my hand up in class. In fact, I hardly understood school and couldn't wait to leave and get on with starting my rock group. Second, this dear man was one of the worst public speakers I had ever heard. But teach me he did – week by week.

Arthur's public speaking lessons bore some unexpected fruit one Sunday evening. A lawyer happened to hear me give a talk to a group of teenagers and for some reason approached me afterwards and asked me if I wanted to train to become a lawyer in his firm. I told him my parents had no money and he said he'd pay for me to go through law school. By the time I was in my early thirties, I was a joint senior partner in a ten-office legal practice, and also lecturing to thousands of lawyers a year on practice management and expansion.

On one occasion, I was asked to give a keynote address at the Law Society Conference in Vienna. Just before I went on stage, I rang Arthur and said, 'I'm about to speak to a thousand lawyers at a conference in Vienna. You taught me to do this.' He replied, 'Did I?' Arthur also taught me another lesson: sometimes coaches can help their charges achieve more than they could ever do themselves. You don't have to think me a better speaker than you, or even a good public speaker, to benefit from this book. You just have to be willing to learn one thing that will make a difference to you.

Over the past fifty years I've had the privilege of speaking in two distinct settings. First, the business world, where I have addressed blue-chip companies, professional bodies, and occasionally national governments. And second, I have spoken extensively in the church world – individual churches, conferences, seminars and events that have a faith dimension. Whichever domain you speak in, I hope this book will be helpful to you.

I write this book in what some have euphemistically called 'the second half' of my life. I think I may be a little nearer the final whistle than even that phrase implies. (I once heard a friend of fifty-six describe himself as 'middle-aged'. Some wit took him up on it and said, 'Really, John? How many people do you know who are a hundred and twelve?') But it is that very realisation that makes me want to pass on practical lessons that I have learnt – some the hard way, and often from those far more gifted than me.

There are many fine books on public speaking and preaching (and in this book I have not sought to elevate one style of preaching above another); they teach exposition, the use of pitch, pause and pace, body language and a hundred other things. I don't for a moment suggest that this short book is a replacement for any of them. But I can at least tell you this: thousands of people have come up to me at the end of my talks and said, 'Thank you – you touched my heart.' Some have written to me many years later to add, 'And you changed my life.' For some reason, I have connected with them. It's no secret that I believe that connection is the very heart of communication.

I have also been involved in the organisation and presentation of thousands of speaking events. That experience has given me many practical insights – particularly with regard to sound and layout of an auditorium – and I hope these may be helpful to those who have the responsibility for maximising an audience's good experience.

As I mentioned earlier, I give examples from my experience of speaking in the business world and in the faith community, but with regard to the latter, I realise, of course, that not all of my readers will share my beliefs. However, I believe that to communicate to others is one of the greatest privileges in the world, and whatever you believe or don't believe, whatever context you speak in, and whatever stage you have reached in your speaking journey, I hope with all my heart that this book will make you even more effective in that calling.

All the great speakers were bad speakers at first.

• • •

Ralph Waldo Emerson

CHAPTER 2

Your Talk: Credibility, Content and Soul

• • •

The ancient Greek philosopher Aristotle suggested that the art of public speaking is essentially the art of persuasion, and that there are three distinct elements which should be at the heart of every speech: ethos, logos and pathos. Let's consider them in turn.

Ethos

Ethos is a Greek word meaning 'character'. In the context of public speaking it answers the question, 'Is this person worth listening to?' or 'What right do they have to give this talk?' In other words, it refers to your character, ethics and believability. If you speak to the same group of people every week, you probably don't need to remind them each time why it is worth their listening to you speak – they made up their mind on that long ago. And the same is true of many other speaking situations. In some cases, the audience have either already decided that you have the right to speak or perhaps they believe it just doesn't matter: if you are giving the address at a wedding, nobody is going to want to know that you are an expert wedding speaker and that this is your twentieth engagement this year.

But in other situations, the element of ethos is absolutely vital. Taking time to establish your credibility – your character – helps put the audience in the right frame of mind to listen to you. The Apostle Paul knew that increasing his credibility with his listeners before and during his talks increased the possibility that they would accept his arguments. Sometimes he kept quiet about his credentials, but at other times he found it helpful to remind his audience of them; he knew that, for at least some, his background and experience would make a big difference.

Imagine that somebody is about to give a talk to a group of business people entitled 'Handling Tensions in the Workplace' – let's call her Claire Hicks. It will help her considerably if the chairperson takes a little time to build her credentials. For example:

Our speaker today worked for many years in the City as an investment banker, then after her ordination she became chaplain to the London Chamber of Commerce. She is the author of *Life Lessons from the Trading Floor*. Ladies and gentlemen, please welcome Claire Hicks!

Ethos does not just achieve the goal of proving you have the right to speak – it can also help create empathy with the audience. Steve Jobs understood this. When he gave his famous commencement speech at Stanford in July 2005, he didn't need to convince them that he was successful. What he was trying to establish was that those achievements had not come easily. He wanted to connect with those students – some of them from challenging backgrounds and with significant struggles ahead – at the start of their entrepreneurial journey:

> Woz and I started Apple in my parents' garage when I was twenty. We worked hard, and in ten years Apple had grown from just the two of us in a garage into a $2 billion company with over four thousand employees. We had just released our finest creation – the Macintosh – a year earlier, and I had just turned thirty . . .*

* Stanford News, Commencement Address at Stanford University by Steve Jobs, CEO of Apple Computers and of Pixar Animation Studios, 12 June 2005.

This is not an easy area to get right. Going over the top with an introduction can alienate an audience. That's why you should never let a chairperson introduce you as 'One of the best/funniest/most motivational speakers' they have ever heard. It makes those who are listening whisper under their breath, 'Oh really? Impress us!' – and it's normally downhill from there. A friend told me the story of a man who was introduced like this: 'Ladies and gentlemen, it's wonderful to have Brett Clevedon with us today. Brett made ten million dollars in oil.' When Brett took the stage he looked as though he was struggling with something, but eventually he spoke. 'I am grateful for that kind introduction, but it wasn't me – it was my brother. And it wasn't oil – it was coal. And he didn't make ten million dollars – he lost it.'

On the other hand, the chairperson who says, 'I'm not going to spend time introducing our speaker today' often does nobody any favours. In those circumstances, you may have to do the credibility thing yourself. It's a good idea to have a short piece you are comfortable with up your sleeve that you can then begin with. It should give people a sense of what you have done in the past but avoid making you look as if you are totally in love with yourself – perhaps something like this: 'Thanks for the opportunity to speak to you today. For the past twenty years I have been involved in education/the third sector/the political arena/church leadership. I hope some of the lessons I've learnt down all those years will be helpful to you today . . .'

Logos

The second element of Aristotle's three modes of persuasion is *logos* – the attempt to convince an audience by an appeal to logic or reason. It means constructing a persuasive argument, organising your various points in a sequence with each point building on the previous one, and might involve giving facts, citing authorities on a subject, using historical and literal analogies, explaining a text or some statistics. For example, a business seminar might contain something like this:

> The global economy faces serious challenges in this century. Its very nature – particularly its inter-connectedness – has caused a number of problems. Many of these are relatively short-term, such as the recent recession following the banking crisis, and often self-correcting. Others, however, have long-lasting effects. The change in oil markets in the 1970s is felt right up to the present time. This

table shows some of those 'global shocks' and their relative longevity.

Or perhaps in a church service:

> In our autumn series on the theme 'You've Got Mail', we are studying some of the letters of the New Testament. Today we are considering Paul's second letter to Timothy. Allow me to give a little background. It was written when Paul was in prison. We can tell that because of Chapter 1:8, 'Do not be ashamed of the testimony about our Lord or of me his prisoner' and also Chapter 1:16, 'Onesiphorus . . . was not ashamed of my chains.' It was certainly written in Rome, but we are not sure exactly when. Paul seems to know that he is near the end of his life. That has led most scholars to believe that this was his second imprisonment and, if so, it was probably written around AD 66 – about thirty-five years after the death of Jesus.

We all learn in different ways and for many people the logical argument, the academic explanation, the evidence for suppositions will be very important, whether, for example, in apologetics, business, education or medicine. In teaching from the text of the Bible, a serious consideration of meanings of its original language, historical context and the writings of scholars we respect will help keep us from purely individualistic interpretations of the passage we are speaking about.

And that brings us to Aristotle's last element of persuasion . . .

Pathos

It is from *pathos* that we get our words 'sympathy' and 'empathy'. Pathos is essentially an appeal to the heart – to the emotions.

On 4 June 1940, Britain was in one of the most difficult periods of its history. Hundreds of thousands of soldiers had just been rescued from the German advances and plucked off the beaches at Dunkirk. France had fallen, and just a tiny strip of water separated a battered country from the most formidable of foes. The previous month, Winston Churchill had faced his cabinet and resisted intense pressure to come to a 'peace settlement' with Hitler. But now he was about to address the House of Commons. It was the darkest hour of the Second World War and he desperately needed to inspire the nation with the hope and courage to fight on.

He could have chosen at that crucial moment to make his appeal by using the element of logos – perhaps reading from reports of his generals or reciting statistics of resistance victory in occupied Europe. But when Churchill stood in the House of Commons on that summer's day it was not to logic or reason that he turned, but to pathos – the emotions:

> Even though large tracts of Europe and many old and famous States have fallen or may fall into the grip of the Gestapo and all the odious apparatus of Nazi rule, we shall not flag or fail. We shall go on to the end. We shall fight in France, we shall fight on the seas and oceans, we shall fight with growing confidence and growing strength in the air, we shall defend our island, whatever the cost may be. We shall fight on the beaches, we shall fight on the landing grounds, we shall fight in the fields and in the streets, we shall fight in the hills; we shall never surrender . . .*

Some say that short speech changed the course of the war.

* House of Commons, *Hansard's Parliamentary Debates: The Official Report* (4 June 1940, vol. 361 cc787-98). https://api.parliament.uk/historic-hansard/commons/1940/jun/04/war-situation.

Before we leave the Houses of Parliament on that auspicious day, if you listen to a recording of that speech you will notice that Churchill employed one of the most effective tools of pathos – pause. At times he took it even further by including moments of silence. As you grow in confidence as a public speaker, try experimenting with this – letting your words hang in the air for a moment before pressing on. The following is a letter I have recited hundreds of times at my events – I know it word for word. It was written to me many years ago by a woman:

Dear Rob, thank you for coming to our city with your seminar; I really enjoyed it. I was a disappointment to my father – he wanted a son. He never hugged me, told me he loved me, or praised me (I think maybe he thought praise would make me big-headed). I know he was a product of his generation, nevertheless my self-esteem is very low. I often feel guilty and very depressed . . .

Whenever I read this letter to an audience, I pause at this point and say, 'And then she wrote this:

"I am eighty-five years old."'

I think that line is so moving that it deserves to hang in the air for a while before I start to speak again.

Silence is powerful. Henri Nouwen said, 'Somewhere we know that without silence words lose their meaning', and at times there can be incredible pathos in simply saying a phrase followed by a short silence to let it sink into an audience's hearts: 'Tomorrow doesn't have to be like yesterday', 'Don't be afraid', 'Don't lose heart.'

I sometimes hear speakers say, 'I don't want to appeal to people's emotions – that's too shallow.' But emotions are part of the way we are designed. Do you not think that Jesus was appealing to the emotions as he told the story of the father running down the road to welcome home his prodigal son?

Ethos, logos and pathos – but which is the most important?

The answer depends on your audience and what you are hoping to achieve in your talk. I used to teach commercial law to postgraduates who were about to become solicitors. There wasn't much need (or opportunity!) for pathos in those lectures. No, the element I needed to utilise, first, was ethos – I had to ensure the students trusted my credentials. And, second, I used logos – they needed sound academic material that would help them pass the impending examinations.

The lecture hall makes it easy to make those choices, but I had a much more complicated tussle with my public speaking style some years later. I'll tell you about this in the next chapter.

Your Talk: Credibility, Content and Soul
CHECKLIST

☐ Remember Aristotle's three pillars of public speaking: ethos, logos and pathos.

☐ Take some time to establish your credibility.

☐ Construct a persuasive argument, organising your various points into a sequence with each point building on the previous one.

☐ Don't be afraid to touch people's emotions.

There are three things to aim at in public speaking: first, to get into your subject, then to get your subject into yourself, and lastly, to get your subject into the heart of your audience.

• • •

Alexander Gregg

CHAPTER 3

Remember You Are Talking to *Ordinary* People

• • •

For a considerable time, I was on the teaching team of quite a large church. The congregation was, to say the least, varied – people from a huge variety of backgrounds, employment situations, intellectual abilities, financial and family circumstances, all sharing church life together. Among this mix of people were a number of academics – several of whom would go on to achieve international repute in the areas of apologetics and biblical studies, and at least six who would become professors, two at Oxford. I was in awe of some of these people. When it was my turn to preach, I would prepare meticulously – often spending hours to put together a thirty-minute talk. At that time I used what, in the legal practice, we called 'counsel's notebooks' – large blue pads to write out every single word that I would say. I still have dozens of these notebooks in my study; they go back over forty years and have titles such as 'Luke 7', 'The Lord's prayer – Our Father', 'Forgiveness' and 'The life of David' scrawled on the covers.

I thank God for those years and the routine of studying, preparing and delivering those talks. The discipline of that teaching team has served me well, but I am sorry to tell you that for many years I think I was often more concerned with what the people I thought of as 'theologians' in the congregation thought of my talks, rather than the vast majority. But one day I had what I can only describe as a revelation: it dawned on me that if I stopped random members of the congregation outside church ten minutes after the service was over and asked them to tell me what I'd been speaking about, many would probably be unable to answer. I was in the high pulpit, they were in the pews beneath, and I hadn't really connected with their everyday lives. In more ways than one, my finely crafted talk had gone over their heads.

Ordinary people

That realisation coincided with my reading a book by the theologian and pastor Professor Lewis B. Smedes, *How Can It Be All Right When Everything Is All Wrong?* He related an incident that occurred as he was about to drive to a small church and be ordained into Christian ministry, something for which he felt fearfully unprepared. As he was about to get into his car, he turned to his friend and former seminary teacher for some final advice:

> 'George, do you have one last good word for me before I take this plunge?' George shot his answer back, as if it had been coiled tight in his mind, the one thing he thought I still needed to know. 'Remember', he said, 'that when you preach, you will be preaching to ordinary people.'
>
> Thanks a lot, I thought. For this kind of wisdom you get to be a professor in a theological seminary? . . . As it turned out, though, in my early years of arrogant innocence, I did not really know much about ordinary people . . . I was ripe with scholarly insights. I was tuned in to my theology. I was tuned in to the craft of sermonising. But I was not tuned in to the ordinariness of the people who listened to my idealistic preaching.

What George was trying to tell me was that a lot of people who would be looking to God for help through me would be ordinary in this sense: they would be living, not on the peak of success, but at the edge of failure; not on the pinnacle of triumph, but at the precipice of defeat. He did not mean that everyone who came to me would be a failure. What he meant was that many of them would feel like failures sometime in their lives. It took me too long to learn how right he was.

They came to my church on Sunday, ordinary people did, but I did not recognize them in the early days. I know now why I did not recognize them; I did not want them to be ordinary people. I wanted them to be harts panting for the water brooks of my sermons. I wanted them to be minds buzzing like souped-up computers digesting my great ideas.

But while I was offering them the precious promises and walloping them with the heroic mandates of the Word of God, many of them were secretly praying, 'O God, I don't think I can get through the week – HELP ME!'

Sometimes, as I sit in a pew and listen to a preacher calling the people to 'let justice roll down like waters, and righteousness like a mighty stream' over the market places and council chambers of every village, or promise the abundant life of joy and peace in the Spirit, I look around. And the dramatis personae, the characters in the churchly scenario, look like this for me:

A man and woman, sitting board-straight, smiling on cue at every piece of funny piety, are hating each other for letting romance in their marriage collapse on a tiring treadmill of tasteless, but always tidy, tedium.

A widow, whispering her Amens to every promise of divine providence, is frightened to death because the unkillable beast of inflation is devouring her savings.

A father, the congregational model of parental firmness, is fuming in the suspicion of his own fatherly failure because he cannot stomach, much less understand, the furious antics of his slightly crazy son.

An attractive young woman in the front pew is absolutely paralyzed, sure she has breast cancer.

A middle-aged fellow who, with his new Mercedes, is an obvious Christian success story, is wondering when he will ever have the guts to tell his boss to take his lousy job and shove it.*

---

* Rob Parsons, *The Book That Changed My Life: How Can It Be All Right When Everything Is All Wrong?* by Lewis B. Smedes, (Authentic Media, 2011).

So what was the phrase that changed the way I would speak in public forever?

'Remember that when you preach, you will be speaking to ordinary people.'

It is easy, even for accomplished speakers (perhaps 'accomplished speakers' especially) to get this wrong. I recently heard a very gifted man speak for an hour. Never mind anything else – his sheer staying power was impressive. But during his talk, as I gazed around the audience, their glazed looks and shuffles hinted that maybe he was not *connecting* with them.

Wanting to reach 'ordinary people' doesn't mean a 'dumbing down' of our talks so that none of it is intellectually challenging. But it does mean at least two things: first, that we want everybody in the audience, irrespective of their IQ, business experience or theological knowledge, to be able to at least get *something* from our talk; and second, an acknowledgement that all of us have needs deeper than purely academic stimulation.

If we want our words to change things for the better for those who listen to us – whether we are trying to help businesses improve customer experience, to motivate volunteers in a political party, or simply hoping that what we say will encourage somebody in their walk of faith – we are going to have to do more than communicate: we're going to need to connect. In the next chapters we are going to talk about that very thing: how to build a strong connection with an audience – how to build a *relationship*.

Remember You Are Talking to *Ordinary* People

CHECKLIST

☐ Check your ego – a highly crafted, erudite and expert talk is no good if it doesn't address the thoughts and concerns of your audience.

☐ This doesn't mean that we have to 'dumb down'. It *does* mean that we want everybody, irrespective of their experience or knowledge, to at least get *something* from our talk.

☐ Acknowledge that all of us have needs deeper than purely academic stimulation.

Designing a presentation without an audience in mind is like writing a love letter and addressing it: To Whom It May Concern.

• • •

Ken Haemer

CHAPTER 4

How to Really Connect with an Audience

• • •

One of the world's most respected leadership experts, John Maxwell said: 'Everyone communicates, few connect.' Here are some ways to achieve that connection.

Know your audience

I love to spend time with people who can help me be a more effective communicator. In fact, about four times a year, I meet with around a dozen men and women who spend their lives in public speaking. We share lessons learnt when our talks seem to have gone well and – far more interesting – when they have gone badly. We talk about what we do when we suddenly dry up or drop our notes. We share with each other how we prepare, practise and mould a talk. Those times are invigorating. I believe one of those people to be one of the most effective communicators I have ever heard, and it was from him that I got a piece of advice that was pure gold. He said that if you really want to connect with the audience there is something you must do before you open your mouth to speak, and preferably before you even start preparing: you have to *know* them.

When I was in my late twenties, I used to speak quite a lot in university discussions and debates. During one of these sessions I used a talk in which I reeled off statistic after statistic about how human life was under threat – ecologically, militarily and from social unrest. The following weekend I was due to speak at a small church on a vast housing estate. I decided to tweak the university talk and use it there. I later discovered that this housing estate was incredibly deprived. The rate of unemployment among those who lived there was sky high, there were almost no facilities, no community centres or even a decent bit of grass for the kids to play on. One woman told me that sometimes people pushed dog excrement through her door. But I knew none of that as I took the pulpit on that Sunday morning and gave my 'The world is in a lot of trouble' talk.

It appeared to go well – although I must say there didn't seem to be the sense of connection with the audience that I have often felt. As I was putting my notes back into order at the end of the service, an elderly lady came up to me. She was tiny, had silver-coloured glasses perched on the end of her nose, a sturdy walking stick – and attitude. I say 'attitude' because that is how it appeared at the time, but as I've thought about what she said to me on that winter Sunday I have been grateful for her words. She said, 'Well done, son. Your talk was fine – except for this: life is hard for the people you spoke to this morning. They don't need somebody telling them how bad the world is – they know that. What they need is a little hope.' And she was right. I hadn't taken the time beforehand to find out even a little about the lives of those who would be listening to me.

Knowing your audience is important. Of course, if you are speaking in the same setting week by week you will generally have an understanding of your listeners' circumstances, but, if not, take time to find out. It's always worth the ten minutes it takes to ring the person who invited you to speak and ask them to tell you about the audience. Try to get an understanding of the diversity of people to whom you will be speaking, and ask what it is the organisers are hoping to get from your visit – get some colour.

Another way to get to know your audience is to meet them. Arrive early and mingle with the delegates or congregation before the event. Those who may not realise that many public speakers are actually introverts cannot understand how this prospect could possibly be so terrifying, but if you can manage it, it is almost always worthwhile. A simple introduction with a handshake – 'Hi, I'm Matt, I'll be speaking a little later on. Have you come far today?' – will normally be enough to start a brief conversation. Just a word of warning, however: don't try to meet the whole audience! It's important to leave enough time to have a moment to sit quietly in the green room or, if there isn't one, the toilet, before you go on. By the way, one speaker told me that she always switches off her mobile phone about an hour before a talk because she's found that it's so easy to be unsettled by a difficult conversation.

Don't waste the start

It may be tempting to ramble a little at the beginning just to get your sea legs, but don't do that:

Good morning. Gosh, I can't remember when I spoke here last – good to see Jim Protheroe in the audience over there – you're looking younger than ever, Jim – and your lovely wife Edna – nice dress, Edna. Well, I wasn't sure what to talk to you about today. I think last time I spoke to you was on the subject of . . .

Instead, try to capture an audience's attention. It could be something like:

Everybody in this auditorium is afraid of something. I wonder what your greatest fear is? Franklin D. Roosevelt said in his first inaugural address, 'The only thing we have to fear is fear itself.' But was he right? I hope by the end of our time together, we'll know the answer to that question.

Or we could begin a talk in a business setting:

Great to be with you today. In over twenty-five years of insolvency work, I have seen time and time again three basic errors in companies that fail. My purpose in speaking to you today is to avoid any one of them destroying *your* business.

Introductions need to be effective, but not too long. Renowned nineteenth-century preacher C.H. Spurgeon summed it up well: 'It is always a pity to build a great porch to a little house.'

Get people on the bus

The memory of one of the first marriage seminars I spoke at is seared into my mind. It was a Saturday event and the morning was split into two one-hour slots. During the first hour, I mentioned, among other issues, the special pressures that having young children can have on a marriage. There was a coffee break between the sessions, and I had only just started sipping my drink in the green room, when a woman burst in. She was red with anger. She said, 'How dare you assume that every married couple has children!' From that day on, I have taken time at the beginning of almost every talk I give to make everybody feel included – to help each person there 'get on the bus'.

I now start a seminar on marriage with something like this:

You are all so welcome today. And, of course, this is a mixed audience. Most of you will be married. Some of your marriages will be wonderful just now – in fact, even as I speak, one of you is gently caressing the hair of the other, and this evening one of you will cook another perfect meal, the glow of the candles promising that the night is far from over. But others of you will be going through tough times in your relationship. In fact, although you are now sitting together, at least one of you feels that it's actually all over. Some of you have just begun a relationship; others have been together for a quarter of a century. Some of you have known the pain of divorce. Some of you have children; others don't. Some of you are just thinking about getting married. All kinds of people are here in all kinds of situations. But I hope that for each of you there will be at least one thing in our short time together that will make a difference for good in your relationships.

Let me give you an example of a 'get them on the bus' opener that I might use if I am running a *Heart of Success* business seminar:

It's good to be with you all today. This is a diverse audience. Some of you, I know, have enormous experience of business. You have built successful companies over many years. Others of you are at the very beginning of your business lives. Just before we began, someone who is fresh out of business school told me, 'I've come to this because I want to avoid the mistakes my dad made. He was very successful, but he lost his family.' Some of you are in massive corporations, others have only one pay cheque to worry about – yours! But we have all come with one thing in common: we are still learning. I would sit in a seminar all day to hear just one good idea that can make a difference – perhaps that will give us a healthier bottom line or improve our family life, time management skills or even our health. I hope with all my heart that whatever your situation, you find that one thing today.

If I'm speaking in a church setting I might start like this:

It's good to be with you all today. I realise that we will all be at different places on our faith journey. Some of you have been Christians for many years; others are just beginning that adventure. Some of you are not at all sure what you believe; others are quite sure that you believe in nothing. Some of you feel so close to God it's almost as if you could reach out and touch him; others of you who were once so sure of what you believed, find now that faith is low in your heart. There are single people here, married people; people going through good times in life and people who are struggling. Some of you have kids who are doing well; others have kids who are breaking their hearts. Young people, older people – all kinds of people at various stages in both their faith and their life journeys. I pray that whatever your situation, you may hear something today that will bring hope and blessing into your life.

If you are speaking in the same church or to the same set of office workers week in week out, you won't want to go through that each time, but it is still helpful to do it once in a while. I find that people will normally forgive you if you don't mention their particular situation in your talk and will interpret what you say to fit them, but it helps if they know you've at least thought about them – that you got them on the bus.

Make them feel welcome

It's easy to alienate members of an audience, and, if we do that, it's almost impossible to build a strong connection with them. Be careful not to do that. If somebody comes in late, resist making a clever comment such as, 'Ah well, better late than never.'

On occasions you might want to let them get off the bus for a while. Perhaps, for example, there are sections of your talk when you know you may be going too deep or technical for some of your audience. At those times it's sometimes helpful to say something like, 'I want to spend a moment going a little deeper and dealing with an aspect of our subject that may not interest everybody. Feel free to switch off for five minutes – I'll tell you when I resurface!' Of course, most people's natural reaction is, 'No – I'm staying with him!'

Don't abuse an audience

Avoid scolding the audience. Sometimes I hear speakers say, 'Good morning!' They get a somewhat half-hearted reply. (Not surprising, as speakers don't look for replies to most things they say.) But then they harangue the audience, 'Come on – you can do better than that! Let's try again!' This time they bellow, 'Good morning!' and get a slightly improved response. 'That's much better!' they say. 'I thought you were all still asleep!'

Don't point. 'If you want to lose weight, it's not rocket science – you need to eat less, eat better and exercise more. You need to be more disciplined!' (said with a forefinger thrust forward). When we do that we are increasing the emotional distance between us and the audience.

Use 'us' and 'we' instead of 'you' and soften injunctions. Let's have another shot at the warning in the paragraph above: 'Of course, there will be those with special medical conditions that affect metabolism, but the simple truth is that for most of us, if we want to be healthy, we have to choose what we eat more carefully and exercise more. I'm sure that like most of us, you may find that hard – it takes real discipline.'

We've established that our goal is not just communication but connection. I believe the next two chapters could help many of us improve that connection by 50 per cent in just six months.

How to Really Connect with an Audience
CHECKLIST

☐ Take ten minutes to ring the person who invited you to speak and ask them about the audience. Try to get an understanding of the diversity of those to whom you will be speaking.

☐ Ask the organiser what they are hoping to get from your visit.

☐ Meet your audience – arrive a little early and mingle.

☐ Don't waste the start. It may be tempting to ramble a little, but aim to capture your listeners' attention immediately.

☐ Get people on the bus. Welcome *everyone*, recognising that all kinds of people in all kinds of circumstances will be in the room.

☐ Don't abuse your audience – for example, by pointing, admonishing. Remember to smile occasionally.

They may forget what you said – but they will never forget how you made them feel.

• • •

Carl W. Buechner

CHAPTER 5

Discover the Power of Stories

• • •

There are moments in all our lives when we feel foolish. We wonder how we could have missed a barn door with such incredible skill. I had that feeling the day I realised that I had missed out on using one of the most potent aids of the public speaker: telling stories.

I know there is a debate as to how much stories should be used in sermons, but, whatever side you take, the simple truth is that properly used stories are powerful. Jesus told lots of them. In fact, he told so many that it was said of him that when he was teaching the crowds who followed him, 'He did not say anything to them without using a parable', and indeed a large proportion of the Gospels are made up of these short stories. As

Jesus told them in the Aramaic tongue of the ordinary people, he captured his audience's imagination – and attention. The stories were varied, but were usually about the everyday affairs of life experienced by his audience – stories about the harvest, wayward children, debt, lost sheep, frustration at the court system, and many others. Jesus understood the power of stories to open people's hearts.

One day, the religious leaders levelled a criticism against Jesus: 'This man welcomes sinners, and eats with them.' Instead of rebutting their complaints with a complicated theological answer, he told them three stories.

The first was about a shepherd who had 100 sheep. As it was getting dark and he was counting them back into the fold, he noticed that one was missing. Ninety-nine out of a hundred is not bad on a cold night in the Judean hills, but it wasn't enough for this particular shepherd: he pulled his cloak around him and went looking for the one lost *away* from home.

The second story had, as its central character, a woman who had ten precious coins and lost one. She turned the house upside down looking for something that was lost *at home.*

And finally Jesus told a story that we call the parable of the prodigal son. Actually, it is a tale of two sons: one who is lost *away* from home and an elder brother, who, because of his attitude, was lost *at* home.

Storytelling is more ancient than fire, and I believe that I improved as a speaker the moment I began to tell stories; not just any story, but stories that can help an audience not only hear what I am speaking about but *feel* it.

The good folk who attended the little chapel on the corner of my street were keen on preaching, and thankfully for me they were willing to give even young guns a try. But they did give me a warning. They said, 'Stories and illustrations must always illuminate the part of the Bible that you are speaking about. You begin with the text and then find the story to illustrate it.'

I think they were right – but only 50 per cent right. Sometimes you can *start* with the story. In a business or education setting we may ask, 'What lessons or principles can we learn from this story?' In a church setting it may be, 'How can I use this story to teach something about the life of faith?' And there are many places from which we can source them: a friend may share an experience, we may come across something on the news, TV and films, social media or the Internet. And when we do hear a story, we should ask ourselves, 'Is there any way I can use this to illuminate what I am trying to say?'

People sometimes say to me, 'You tell so many stories – where do you get them all?' I watch. Over many years I have developed a 'filter' that has helped me spot situations and stories that I know I will be able to use. And when I see or hear something that can help me convey a business principle or encourage someone in a family seminar, I do three things: I record it. I practise it. I try it.

In my book *Let Me Tell You A Story* I share forty-nine (don't ask me why I didn't just make it fifty – I have thought the same myself!) of the stories I have told down the years. The truth is there could probably have been 149. These are stories that people have read and passed on to me and personal stories from my own life or the experiences of others who have shared them with me.

When you tell a story during a talk consider the following three elements: detail, empathy, and application.

Detail

Painting in some detail allows the listener to enter more easily into the experience – to imagine that they were there. When he was telling the story of the prodigal son, Jesus inserted this little detail: he was so hungry that 'he longed to fill his stomach with the pods that the pigs were eating.' I have often imagined that scene in the pigsty and pictured that young man at the very lowest moment of his life, just before he decided to start the long walk back to his father.

Empathy

Stories are powerful because they allow the listener to put themselves in the picture. We want the audience to feel empathy with the characters – in fact, it is empathy that makes the stories so powerful. Henri Nouwen said that with regard to the parable of the prodigal son 'Sometimes I am the father filled with love for the wayward son, sometimes I am the elder brother with his hard heart and judgemental spirit, and sometimes I look at the dirty, tear-stained face coming down the road towards the house and I know in my heart that I am the prodigal.'

Application

Sometimes applying the message from the story can be done by the speaker, but often it can be left to the listener to find it – it is occasionally more powerful then.

I will never forget speaking at a company's annual conference. Their chartered accountant was sitting in the front row and from the second I started he looked bored – as though much of what I was talking about was beneath him. I had decided to use a very moving story to end and, to be honest, his attitude caused me to reconsider; I wondered if he would think it too emotional, but I decided to tell it anyway. In the middle of that story, I saw him reach into his pocket for his handkerchief and brush away a tear. Something in that story applied to his life and it touched him deeply.

And I have discovered over the years that sometimes saying the simplest things with passion and feeling can reach people in all kinds of situations. Some time ago, I was speaking at a church service and mentioned the poem that I included at the end of my book *The Sixty Minute Father*. It is about a man teaching his small daughter to ride a bicycle – something many of us have done with a child. He holds the back of the saddle when she wobbles, and when she gets a little more confident he lets go. But it doesn't go well for this little girl and in the poem she is trudging home with tears streaming down her face, pushing her bike as her friends whizz by on theirs. But the last verse is different. I always knew that if my daughter Katie asked me to speak at her wedding reception, I would recite that last verse, and I did:

Tomorrow, though, I will run behind,
Arms out to catch her, she'll tilt then balance wide
Of my reach, till distance makes her small.
. . . I stop and know
That to teach her I had to follow
And when she learned, I had to let her go.*

At the end of the service, a woman approached me. She said, 'I found that poem very moving. I wanted to learn to ride a bike when I was a child, but my father refused to hold the back of the saddle. Instead he would just push me – quite hard – and shout, "Pedal!" I often fell off and sometimes cried, but he said I would learn better that way . . . I never did get to learn to ride a bicycle.'

On the following Saturday I was speaking at a conference and during the interval a woman came over and told me she was a counsellor. She said, 'Last Sunday you spoke to one of my clients. She said that if I got the chance to speak with you today, I should tell you something. She had an abusive father, and week by week she comes into my counselling room and talks to me about him. She sits with her arms wrapped tightly around her,

* Poem adapted from 'Learning The Bicycle (for Heather)' by Wyatt Prunty, *The American Scholar*, 58, 1, 1989, p. 122.

but in all the times we have met I have never seen her cry – except this week. When she told me about the poem you read, I saw a tear form in the corner of her eye. I think it might be the beginning of her healing.'

I had told a simple story of a child learning to ride a bicycle – but perhaps it changed somebody's life for ever.

May I share with you two stories I have used many times over the years? As you read them consider the three elements I've mentioned: detail, empathy, and application. The first was told to me by a man I met when I was on a lecture tour in Canada. I call it *Bearer of Hope*.

Bruce, a friend of mine, has a wonderful Christmas memory from when he was a boy. He was born in Northern Ontario, Canada, where the winters are traditionally cold and snowy. His home was an isolated farm, deep in the heart of the country. Several miles further on was a dwelling that enjoyed even greater isolation. It was inhabited by an old recluse called Joe. If anybody wanted to visit Joe (and most people didn't!) they had better be ready for a trek through the woods. Apparently Joe was something of a local mystery – most adults found it easier to ignore him and most kids were in awe of him. Wild stories were passed from child to child about the number of kids Joe had eaten alive, and rumour had it that if he caught you within a mile of his place you would disappear for ever.

Every Christmas, for as long as he could remember, Bruce's father, Don, had trudged through the woods to Joe's cottage to give him some Christmas gifts and, as he put it, 'to let the old boy know that somebody cares'.

Bruce told me he could remember what happened on Christmas Eve 1958 as though it was yesterday. The night before, new snow had blanketed their valley and then the weather had turned clear and cold. Bruce had shivered as he came downstairs and found his father making breakfast beside the old stove. His dad turned to him and said, 'In a moment I'm going to make my trip to Joe's place. Would you like to come with me? I'm carrying quite a bit and I'd appreciate the help.' Bruce said it was hard to believe that his own father wanted him to be eaten alive, but he was torn – no child had ever visited the cottage. He said he'd go.

They walked for thirty minutes or so, their boots making fresh prints in the virgin snow, and then his father pointed to a thin wisp of smoke curling up from the centre of the wood. They waded through knee-deep snowdrifts and, finally, panting and exhausted, knocked on Joe's door. Bruce's heart was pounding in his chest.

The door was opened not by a monster but by an old man with holes in his clothes and a gruff voice that welcomed them in. They entered a one-roomed house that had seen better days and was filled with the smell of a hardwood fire and the unmistakable waft of body odour and old tobacco. Bruce's father set the bags of groceries they'd hauled through the snow onto a sticky oilcloth-covered table near where Joe invited them to sit.

Bruce watched, wide-eyed, while the men made small talk, discussing the recent turn in the weather and whether there would be enough wood to last the winter. After all the local topics had been well covered, Bruce's father said, 'Well, Joe, Christmas is here again and our family just wanted you to have a few groceries as our gift to you. Merry Christmas, Joe!'

And then Bruce's young eyes saw something he has never forgotten. A single tear began to roll down Joe's face and into his thick bushy beard. The old recluse brushed it away with the back of a dirty hand as he mumbled his thanks. Bruce's father said that it was time they were going and shook Joe's hand as they rose and made for the door. Just as they were about to step out into the snow, Joe reached out, touched his father's arm and said, 'Don, you are a bearer of hope.'

It was the last Christmas Eve journey they made to Joe. He died the following January.

As Bruce told me that story, I knew immediately that I would use it. I tried to remember the little details that would bring it to life as I told it: the fresh snow blanketing the valley, seeing the smoke curl up from the centre of the wood, the smell of body odour and old tobacco. When I tell it, I want the audience to have a sense of empathy with the small boy as he sat in Joe's house, and I want them to be able to feel something of what the child felt as he saw the tear roll down Joe's face. The application has not been difficult – something along these lines: 'Ladies and gentlemen, what an incredible thing – to live our lives so that we can be a bearer of hope.'

The second story is a personal one. I have told it many hundreds of times all over the world. I have no doubt that some of my readers can say it with me!

One night just before Christmas, when Dianne and I had been married for just a couple of years, there was a knock on our door. When I opened it, a man was standing there in the darkness. He was holding a frozen chicken in one hand and a black plastic bag in the other, which we later discovered contained all his worldly possessions.

I thought I recognised him. His name was Ron and when we were kids he used to come to our Sunday school. He was slightly educationally challenged and lived in a children's home. Every Sunday, Mr Harker, our Sunday school superintendent, used to collect Ron from the children's home and bring him to the little church on the corner of my street. Now he was in his late twenties. I said, 'It's Ron, isn't it?' He nodded. 'How did you know where we live?' He started to explain, but then I stopped him talking and simply invited him in. Ron had fallen on very hard times. I am sure that those who looked after him in the children's home had done their best for him; nevertheless, at the age of sixteen he'd had to leave and try to make his way in the world with almost no support and few skills – social or otherwise. He was now living in appalling conditions.

'Where did you get your frozen chicken, Ron?' I asked him. He told us that somebody had given it to him as a Christmas present. 'Do you know how to cook it?' I asked. He shook his head vigorously. Dianne took the chicken from his hands and said, 'I'll cook it – and why don't you stay with us tonight?' We found him some pyjamas and toiletries and settled him into our spare room. He stayed with us the next night as well and the night after that. On the third day Dianne said, 'It's Christmas Eve, Ron. Don't leave tonight.'

On Christmas Day Ron joined us for lunch with a few other family members (this was before we had children). We had hastily wrapped a few presents for him, and he shared in the distribution of gifts when the meal was over. He cried. He had never known a family Christmas.

That day was forty years ago, and since then we've had two children. They are grown and gone now with children of their own, but Ron has never left us and, short of needing more care than we are able to give him, he never will.

When he'd been with us a short time, he got a job as a dustman. In those days, I was a young lawyer and on the way to the office I would drop Ron off for work at the refuse depot. When I got home in the evening, Ron would often be sitting in the same chair, smiling away to himself. One night I asked him what it was that amused him so much. He said, 'When you drop me off at work in the mornings, the other men say, "Who's that who brings you to work in the car?" and I say, 'Oh, that's my solicitor!'

I'm sure you can see for yourself the detail, and I hope you have some empathy with Ron, so let me go straight to the final point – application – and how I have often used that story to illustrate the need we all have; the need for somebody to really care:

> I have thought so much about that exchange with Ron. It wasn't that he was being driven to work by a lawyer (who'd be proud of that?). No. I think what was giving Ron so much joy went far deeper than that. He had never had a mum lead him by the hand into the playground on his first day of school. He had never had a dad say when he was 11, 'How was your first day in the big school, son?' And now he was a man – but, for the first time ever, somebody was at the gate. Ladies and gentlemen – we all need somebody at the gate.

As we come to the end of the topic of storytelling, let me leave you with two warnings. The first is not to lose your stories; they are precious – record them as soon as you can. I have often reached for my mobile phone in the middle of the night to capture a story I'd forgotten to record during the day. (I have to say that Dianne is often less impressed by this dedication than I am.) Second, don't tell other people's personal stories as though they have happened to you. If you hear a speaker tell a brilliant story about a hilarious moment in their family life it's tempting to steal it, but don't – not least because it can go very wrong. Some years ago at a large convention a main-platform speaker told a very funny story about a lost rabbit in his home. The audience was rolling in the aisles. The following night another speaker, who hadn't been there the previous evening, told exactly the same story as if it had happened in his home (perhaps it had!) and looked visibly thrown when he didn't get the roars of laughter he expected.

A good way to end a talk

Finally, a story, particularly an uplifting one, is a good way to end a talk. Here's one I have used dozens of times to finish a presentation to business people. It's obviously not a true story and the audience know that, but it is nevertheless effective in making a concluding point.

Many years ago in the Rhondda Valley, there was a baker – Dai Jones. The name of his shop was written proudly above the door: 'Dai the Bread'.

One day a terrible thing happened to Dai. Tesco got planning consent to build a multistorey superstore on his left-hand wall. This colossus of the food business towered into the sky selling all manner of things and, of course, bread – heavily discounted.

Dai's profits plunged, but he worked longer hours, cut margins, and somehow managed to keep going. But then further tragedy struck. Sainsbury's built a 20-storey superstore on his right-hand wall – again selling all manner of goods, including bread – discounted even further.

That night, Dai and his wife, Doris, sat in front of the coal fire in their tiny cottage and discussed what they could do. Dai sighed, 'It's no good, Doris; we'll have to sell the shop and move out of the valley – we've had a good run.' Doris looked crestfallen and then she had an idea. That idea eventually turned them into multimillionaires. When people walked down the village high street the following Wednesday they noticed that Dai's shop window now displayed not just bread but quite a wide variety of groceries. And they also saw that the old sign 'Dai the Bread' had been taken down and a huge new one in neon lights had been put in its place that read: 'ENTRANCE'.

And then I say something like this to apply the story:

Ladies and gentlemen, it's been a privilege to speak to you today. We cannot work in the world of business without facing challenges – including the prospect of being eaten by fish much larger than us – but I wish you the resilience, courage and inspiration of . . . Dai the Bread.

But if believing in the power of stories is one element of improving as a public speaker, the next, for many of us, will be far harder to put into practice.

CHECKLIST

☐ Be a watcher – make it your business to garner stories from your own and others' experiences.

☐ Don't lose your stories – record them as soon as you can, even if you are not sure exactly how and when you will use them.

☐ Remember the key elements in a story – detail, empathy and application.

☐ A story is often a good way to end a talk – it's useful to have a couple in your back pocket.

Reports convey information. Stories create experience. Reports transfer knowledge. Stories transport the reader, crossing boundaries of time, space, and imagination. The report points us there. The story puts us there.

• • •

Roy Peter Clark

CHAPTER 6

Trade Length for Effectiveness

• • •

How long should a sermon or presentation be? The right answer is: as long as it takes to communicate the material effectively. It's a myth that people can't listen to talks longer than ten minutes without getting bored, but it's also strange that in many churches the sermon is thirty minutes long without fail every week. It's also true that some speakers wear their ability to speak for vast periods of time as a badge of honour.

If you're ever invited to give a TED Talk (a video created from a presentation at the main TED – technology, entertainment, design – conference or one of its satellite events) then as well as your best face and finest speech, there's something else you're going to need to pack: your watch. No matter whether you are a famous actor, Nobel Prize winner or simply someone with an incredible story to tell, TED will allocate you eighteen minutes – dead.

According to TED Talks' curator, Chris Anderson, eighteen minutes is 'short enough to hold people's attention and precise enough to be taken seriously. But it's also long enough to say something that matters.'

I don't know if that length is right for the talks you give, but I do know that you can say a lot in that amount of time – and that sometimes it's a good discipline to try to do just that. I am equally aware that there are preachers both current and in history that have given very effective long sermons. I have sat at the feet of some of the greatest preachers of my generation – in one case, literally. I was allowed to perch on the pulpit steps once when Dr Martin Lloyd-Jones was preaching and every seat in the church was taken. Preachers like these can hold people's attention for forty-five minutes without breaking a sweat. But although we might well wish to emulate their style, we would be unwise to think this meant we could speak for as long as they do, or to fall into the misguided belief that length equals authority, spirituality – or effectiveness. Spurgeon, 'the Prince of Preachers', often spoke for a long time, but when he was addressing his students he said,

There is such a thing as having too much to say, and saying it until hearers are sent home loathing rather than longing . . . If you ask me how you may shorten your sermons, I should say *study them better*. Spend more time in the study that you may need less in the pulpit.

On occasions, a short sermon – even a very short one – can be very effective. I remember a dramatic occasion when that happened, I suspect, by accident. The evening service started at 6.30 p.m., and the minister would normally begin preaching at about 7.00 p.m. and end after thirty to forty minutes. One Sunday evening, three young nurses were being interviewed before the sermon. They were leaving their safe and secure jobs in a local hospital to go to a war-torn area of Africa. As they told their story, I think all our hearts were deeply moved. The only problem was that the interview went on longer than planned, so by the time the minister got up to speak it was gone 7.30 p.m. We all thought we were in for a late night, but in fact we got home early.

He entered the pulpit and then said: 'We have been studying the Ten Commandments over the last few weeks and tonight we come to the commandment "You shall not covet". In the light of what we have heard this evening from these young nurses, how dare we covet? Our final hymn is . . .'

That evening service took place over forty years ago, but I have never forgotten that talk.

When I was younger, I used to be very concerned about the amount of time allocated to me to speak. If the chairperson was meant to get me on my feet by seven o'clock and I was still sitting in my seat at ten past, I'd start getting hot under the collar. To be honest, these days I don't. It may be unhelpful or even rude not to give a speaker his or her allocated time, but, if that happens, I try to speak for whatever time I've got left – I imagine the audience don't want to be kept late just because somebody got the timings wrong. Once, after having driven three hours to get to an event, I ended up speaking for just ten minutes.

If you are invited to speak at an event involving a meal, I can tell you that most organisers underestimate how long it will take to serve the food, and often the time for the speech is squeezed. I remember one such event when I was due to speak at 9 p.m. for thirty minutes, but at 9.45 they were just starting to serve the desserts. It's hard to do much about this if you are an invited speaker with no real control over the programme, but if you suspect there may be a problem, one option is to suggest having the speech between the main course and dessert.

It can be annoying to have the time allocated to your talk squeezed, but, once in a while, regard it as a positive challenge to see if you can say something useful in whatever time you've got. A couple of years ago, a radio station asked me to do a series of sixty-second commentaries. After I'd delivered them and realised what you could get into sixty seconds it helped me be a little less screwed up about the ten minutes I was left with once at the end of a dinner.

I honestly have little enthusiasm for entering the debate as to whether talks or sermons should be shorter or longer, but I would say this: within the bounds of the time allocated to you – experiment. There are occasions when we may need a good chunk of time to develop a theme or deliver some teaching effectively, but don't begin preparing as if you have to fill thirty or forty minutes. Most of us will not be in a university setting where lectures need to cover the course curriculum over a precise period of time. I've heard people who preach very long sermons say, 'Ah, but our people would feel cheated if I spoke for less than three quarters of an hour. They appreciate deep teaching.' Comments like that betray pride – and a mistaken view that length equals depth. But worse than that, my fear is that we have started to care too much about the few; we have forgotten the words of that old theology professor: 'Remember that when you preach, you will be preaching to ordinary people.'

At least once in a while – speak shorter.

Everything we have covered so far can increase a sense of connection with our audience, but the principles in the next chapter have the power to take that connection to a new level.

Trade Length for Effectiveness
CHECKLIST

☐ The right length of a talk is as long as it takes to communicate the material effectively.

☐ Don't wear your ability to speak for vast periods of time as a badge of honour.

☐ When the time allocated for your talk has got squeezed, regard it as a positive challenge to see if you can say something useful in whatever time you've got.

☐ At least once in a while, speak shorter.

My job is to talk; your job is to listen. If you finish first, please let me know.

● ● ●

Harry Herschfield

CHAPTER 7

Create a Sense of Intimacy

• • •

I believe that effective public speakers often generate something that you might think is almost impossible in a large audience (and by that I mean anything from fifty to five thousand people): they create a sense of intimacy. When this occurs, the speaker and the audience in some way become one. The listeners are not being lectured to, harangued or even simply taught: they are on a journey with the speaker. In this chapter, I want to suggest three ways to achieve that.

1. 'It was as if he was speaking just to me . . .'

Do you remember that on the first page of this book I spoke about going to a seminar on public speaking and hearing the speaker say two things that impacted me greatly? The first was that we will lose people's attention for two reasons: because we're boring and because we're interesting. The second was this: the greatest compliment you can pay another person when you are talking with them is *to look in their eyes*.

This means that we don't stare at the television to the side of someone, look at the more interesting person who has just joined the party or sneak a glance at our watch. When we look into someone's eyes, we say 'You matter to me', and that gives an incredible sense of connection. Whether we are speaking to a youth group of twenty or to five thousand people in the Royal Albert Hall, we have to try to replicate that sense of intimacy. That's relatively easy if we are speaking to just a few people – perhaps in a book-club or home-group discussion – but we have to do our best in larger settings too. Some speakers look 'over' an audience, but that's not what oratory is about. If it were, we could simply hand out printed notes of our talk. No – when we stand in front of an audience, we are seeking connection and, for that, the eyes are vital.

Other speakers suggest that the way to get this connection is to deliver a few sentences to a particular person in the audience and then direct the next few sentences to someone else – each time keeping eye contact. So for example:

One of the greatest issues facing the business community is the challenge of change.

Delivered to the woman sitting in the third seat along in the front row.

It could be change brought about by technology, the growth of competition in the global village, or the relentless march of regulation. But whatever it is, you'd better believe it – change is here to stay! *Delivered to the man with the red shirt on the left of the aisle.*

Personally I don't like this. I find it awkward for both myself and the unfortunate person in the audience to have that level of eye contact. I prefer a brief moment of eye contact with one person and then to move on to another person in the audience. My friend John Archer, who is a comedy magician, imagines strings coming towards him – not from individuals but from sections of the audience (perhaps groups of twenty or so people). So he moves his head and eyes to the back, to the centre, to the left, the right and the front of the audience. However we do this, the aim is to make every person feel as if we are speaking to them.

When it comes to keeping eye contact with your audience, there are three things worth remembering. First, don't forget the people in the balcony, especially if there are only a few up there. Second, if it's an auditorium with stage lights, it's quite possible that because the lights are in your eyes, you'll only be able to see the front row of the audience – everything else will be in total darkness. You have to remember that although the stage lights have blinded you to them, everybody in the auditorium can see *you* clearly. Make them feel connected to you by looking around the auditorium and imagining the eyes. It's also often useful to move your body slightly, as well as your head, so that the audience can actually see that you are trying to connect with them. And finally, if you are speaking at a large event where a camera is projecting an image of you on to a screen at the front, remember that if you ever want to look right into the eyes of every person listening, you simply have to look straight into the camera lens. They will feel as if they are the only person there.

Keeping our eyes on the audience matters. In the next chapter we will consider what happens when we take our eyes *off* them.

2. Imagine it's a dialogue

Public oratory is, in some ways, unnatural. People sit, often in rows, and one person speaks to them, frequently without there ever being any actual oral interaction between them. Because of this, an effective public speaker has to imagine the comments and questions coursing through their listeners' minds and try to address them. James Comey, former head of the FBI, sums up the attitude we need to achieve this: 'I see this as the heart of emotional intelligence, the ability to imagine the feelings and perspective of another "me"'.

Good public speaking is a two-way conversation with the speaker playing both parts. So, if you are addressing a business audience on the subject of parenting and work-life balance, you might say something like this:

Many people tell me that they don't have time for much family life because they are working hard so that their families can enjoy the things that they themselves didn't have. But don't let that be an excuse for missing your kids' young lives. When it comes to children, the days are long but the years are short. One psychologist put it well: 'Sometimes we are so busy trying to give our kids what we didn't have that we don't have time to give them what we *did* have.'

That's one side of the conversation, but an effective speaker will be able to imagine somebody in the audience saying to themselves, 'That's all very well for him, but since my partner died/we've got into trouble with the mortgage/I'm helping my oldest daughter through college, I really do have to work long hours.' Empathy like that will allow the speaker to add, 'Of course, there may be times in our lives when we simply have to put in those extra hours. All I'm saying is don't let this become a lifestyle for no good reason.'

Or imagine you are speaking in a church on the topic of prayer. You may say, 'God answers prayer!' But somebody in the audience will be saying under their breath, 'Well, he didn't answer my prayer. My husband never recovered from the accident/I still can't get a job/My son still won't speak to me.' A wise speaker will at least acknowledge those unspoken questions.

3. Don't be afraid to be vulnerable

Many years ago, I was invited to speak at a family conference in Scotland on the topic of pressures on the modern family. Around three hundred doctors and social workers would be attending, and I'd be sharing the platform with a theologian. I had been given forty-five minutes for my slot. About six weeks before the event, I was in my study preparing my talk and Dianne came in. She said, 'Why don't I come with you to Scotland and give my perspective on family life?' I was, as my kids used to put it, 'gobsmacked'. I said, 'Di, you have never spoken in public – not even to ten people! How on earth would you do it?' She replied, 'I've been thinking about it, and I think I'll be fine. Why don't you ask the organisers?' So I did. They didn't ask me if she'd ever spoken in public before, and I didn't tell them.

I remember the day well – even now. The theologian spoke for forty-five minutes. I spoke for thirty minutes, and then I said, 'And now ladies and gentlemen, I'd like you to welcome my wife, Dianne.' I had no idea what she was going to say during the fifteen minutes that were left.

Over the last thirty years, I have heard Dianne repeat the words with which she began her short talk that day at many other locations. She has said them at conferences in The Royal Albert Hall, Symphony Hall in Birmingham, The Waterfront Centre in Belfast, and the Scottish Exhibition Centre. She has said them in the USA, Africa, Asia and across Europe. She has spoken to tens of thousands of people. She began like this:

It was, in so many ways, a perfect autumn morning. The sun was streaming through the bedroom windows, I had a lovely daughter of three years old, a newborn son, a lovely home, and I was lying next to my husband who loved me. The only problem was that I had just whispered to Rob, 'Could you take Katie to nursery today? I don't think I can cope anymore.'

Dianne went on to describe the long period of illness that followed – including postnatal depression – and some lessons that we learnt as a couple over those dark years.

When she finished speaking, people applauded loudly and the chairperson brought the formal part of the day to a conclusion. As is common, members of the audience came forward to ask the speaker questions or give comments. And that's when I saw the sight that even now brings a smile to my face: a number of people gathered around the theologian, hardly anybody around me – and a huge crowd surrounding Dianne. Vulnerability is powerful.

Of course, we can't wear our hearts on our sleeves all the time. Nevertheless, it is extremely powerful when a speaker allows an audience to see some inner part of their life; people admire you for your strengths but connect with you in your weaknesses.

Connection illusions

As I close this section, let me say that there are times in public speaking when it seems to be going badly. Never mind creating intimacy, we don't seem to be connecting with an audience at all. But a little warning – it's easy to be fooled. Don't be thrown by the two big connection illusions: corporate reaction and individual reaction.

Let's take corporate reaction first. Imagine the scene. You are ten minutes into your talk, but you feel as if you are dying on stage: there is almost no audience reaction. Jokes that on other occasions have had people rolling in the aisles are coming down from 30,000 feet in balls of fire and exploding on the podium. No matter how scary, moving or motivational the stories you tell, you simply cannot bring this audience to life.

Of course, you may be having a bad day and your communication skills have deserted you, but before you despair and hang up your microphone forever, consider the following. Were the audience comfortable – were they too hot or too cold? Were they stressed when they arrived – perhaps delayed by traffic? And especially consider the audience size in relation to the size of the auditorium. I've never been able to prove it, but I wouldn't mind betting there's a mathematical equation that can work out audience reaction from the size of the venue divided by the number of people there. If you have fifty people in a 500-seater auditorium, no matter how good a speaker you are, it will be a tough job to get a brilliant audience reaction. So often in those situations, the small number of people who are there simply don't have the confidence to respond out loud – but that doesn't mean they are not responding *inside.*

Let's look at the second connection illusion: individual reaction. It's not uncommon for somebody in the audience to scowl at you the whole way through your talk, or perhaps for somebody to smile constantly at you as if they just want to eat you up. The first kind can really throw you. If you are unwise, you try everything to win them around only to discover afterwards that they always look grumpy – it wasn't personal. And the smiler? The one hanging on your every word? Well they always wear that fixed smile. Quite possibly, they haven't listened to a word you've said.

Of course, when presentations go badly there needs to be some in-depth evaluation of why that happened, but the time for that is not during the talk – it's all too easy to come to the wrong conclusion! On seminar tours, I may deliver basically the same material many times, so when there's a difficult audience response, it's easier to push through if, on the previous occasions, listeners have connected well. If twenty other audiences have reacted positively, it is unlikely that the fault is with the material. But whether it's an old talk or a new one, and whether the disappointing reaction is individual or corporate, you just have to hold your nerve. Keep going with your material and you'll often find that when people speak with you afterwards they were with you all along. The smaller audience who didn't react openly, enjoyed the event just as much as the massive crowd who cheered, laughed and clapped through your whole presentation.

In this chapter, we have considered ways to connect on a very deep level with an audience so that people begin to feel that you are speaking just to them. But even if we achieve communication at this level, it's very hard to sustain it. At the beginning of this chapter we looked at the importance of eye contact. In the next few chapters we will look at some of the great distractors that make it hard to keep that deep sense of connection. And, for a while, we will stay with the theme of eyes.

Create a Sense of Intimacy
CHECKLIST

☐ Seek connection by looking into your audience's eyes.

☐ Imagine it's a dialogue. Think about the comments and questions that are coursing through your listeners' minds and try to address them.

☐ Don't be afraid to be vulnerable. We can't wear our hearts on our sleeve all the time, but it's extremely powerful when a speaker allows an audience to see some inner part of their life.

Those who are willing to be vulnerable move among mysteries.

• • •

Theodore Roethke

CHAPTER 8

Notes or No Notes?

• • •

Public speakers like Barack Obama have popularised speaking without notes and it's not hard to see why: every time we look down at our notes we lose eye contact with our audience – and, therefore, risk losing their attention. If you can copy Obama and still speak effectively then no doubt it's the best way. But the key word here is 'effectively'. In 2014, Ed Miliband, who was then leader of the Labour party, got into a spot of bother at the party's conference when he spoke without notes and omitted two very important policy statements, one on immigration and the other on the budget deficit.

If we *can* manage not to miss out vital elements of our talk, then the main thing we achieve when we don't use notes is increased connection with our listeners. Perhaps the most famous occasion of somebody connecting with their audience by discarding their notes successfully occurred on the steps of the Lincoln Memorial in Washington DC on 28 August 1963. Dr Martin Luther King, Jr looked out on a crowd of 250,000 faces, many of whom had been subject to beatings, shootings and systematic prejudice because of the colour of their skin. They brought their grievances to the capital and looked to their leader to inspire them with hope. He began reading from his handwritten draft, but he was just not managing to connect fully with the vast, expectant crowd. As he was nearing the end of his set speech, the famous gospel singer Mahalia Jackson shouted out, 'Tell them about the dream, Martin!' Dr King heard her, pushed his notes aside, and delivered one of the most memorable speeches in human history.

I have watched the film of that occasion time and time again. I find it fascinating to compare the change in the listeners' demeanour before and after Dr King pushes his notes aside and speaks from his heart. Beforehand, the audience looks listless and, at times, even bored; afterwards they become animated and impassioned. But there is an even more fascinating change: it is in Luther King himself. When he begins to speak extemporaneously, he comes alive, feeding off the positive connection with his audience. In a moment of pure magic, speaker and listeners become one.

So should it be with or without notes? In the end, we must decide what works for us – and it may differ from talk to talk. If we are a church leader giving a new talk every week we may feel it isn't a good use of time to memorise our sermon. On the other hand, if we're using a similar talk in various settings, then putting the time in so that we don't have to rely on notes may be worthwhile.

Personally, I think that although speaking totally without notes is, as in Martin Luther King's experience, often effective (and certainly impressive) it is sometimes neither wise nor necessary. However, if we do decide to use notes, we must remember that constantly looking at them will normally make it harder to stay connected to our audience. Unless we are speaking in an academic setting where the imparting of information is primary, we will often want to touch people's hearts as well as their heads. For that, eye contact is vital.

When it comes to solving the notes or no notes dilemma, I can tell you what works for me. I start by reading around the subject (one brilliant speaker told me that the well should always be deeper than the bucket!), and then I type out my talks word for word. When I've worked on the presentation – edited it a little and tweaked here and there – I put a pile of books on the desk in my study to act as a lectern and I read the talk out loud. I do this exactly as if I was giving it in real life, including, 'It's good to be with you today at the Manchester Chamber of Commerce.' And as I say it aloud, I listen. I know, by now, that the talk works as a piece of prose, but does it work when spoken?

When I was a student, I had an old banger of a car. In those far-off days, there were things like plugs, points and carburettors, and a combination of malfunction on any of those three (and, on occasion, all three together) would give you a 'flat spot'. I'd be overtaking, there would be a lorry coming towards me, I'd push my foot harder on the accelerator, but nothing would happen. When I'm saying my talks out loud in my study, I sometimes hit a 'flat spot' – I can sense it. This is a moment in the presentation when it's like ploughing through treacle. Or, to change the metaphor, the talk becomes too stuffy and it's time for me to open a window and let in some air. At this point, I need to insert a story or other illustration, or, at the very least, change pace. Those who teach aspiring authors often tell them to 'Kill your darlings'. It simply means to cut away parts of your writing – anecdotes, turns of phrase – that you might love but do not advance what you are trying to say. It hurts, but sometimes you have to do it. So how can we spot our 'darlings' in order to dispense with them? One way is by *listening* to our own talks.

Be your own audience

In Care for the Family we use a personality profiling tool called The Birkman Method. I'm sure many of you will have undergone similar tests to help both you and employers discover your strengths and gifting. When my report came, Dianne and I sat down together to look at it. It seemed to hold few surprises apart from one: it gave me a high 'musical' score. Dianne teased me about that report for years because the truth is that I don't have a wide taste in music and don't have much rhythm (a guest at a wedding once likened my dancing to a demented turtle's efforts to right itself). However, a few years ago, Dianne and I got a bit of a shock. I had just finished speaking in a large auditorium in South Africa, and as I was about to leave, a woman approached me. After some pleasantries, she asked, 'Are you a musician?' I said, 'No, definitely not.'

'Oh,' she said, 'I'm surprised. I'm a professor of music and listening to you speak is like listening to a piece of music. You have a cadence of language – your presentation had a rhythmic flow of sounds.'

Nowadays, when I am in my study practising, I listen for those rises and falls. I listen for the flat spots. I listen for the parts where the talk becomes stuffy, and I can sense that, unless I change it, the audience will be crying out for air. I listen.

I also find it helpful to ask somebody whose opinion I value to listen to a new talk before I actually deliver it live. If you can find a suitable mentor, and you have the teachable spirit that I spoke about at the beginning of the book, you will see enormous benefit from doing this. I realise this is harder if you are giving a new talk every week, but even then I would urge you to do it when you can.

When I have made whatever changes I think are needed, I try to reduce the talk to headings with paragraphs and then I practise it again. I will then reduce it to bullet points, putting them on a card and writing out underneath them any statistics or quotes that I want to make sure I get right. Trust me – if I could be sure I'd never need them, I'd dispense even with those bullet points, because I know that every time I take my eyes off the audience I lose something of a connection. But even the most proficient public speakers can experience their mind going blank and – although I sometimes decide not to use any notes at all – for me, my bullet points are usually a price worth paying.

Finally, I practise, often going through a talk time and time again in my study. I know this is not always possible if you have to give several new talks a week, but even then you may be able to give some special attention to the beginning and the end, which are often crucial for your confidence. Those practice sessions allow me to use my notes as little as possible. When I stand up in front of that audience I want to connect with them and in order to do that I must, as far as possible, keep my eyes on them.

We have talked about the importance of keeping our eyes on the audience, but in the next chapter we turn to another problem: *when your listeners take their eyes off you.*

Notes or No Notes?
CHECKLIST

☐ Every time we look down at our notes, we risk losing our listeners' attention. But speaking without notes risks floundering and missing out some important points.

☐ Whether or not you use notes, remember that eye contact is vital.

☐ Practise your talk. Listen for rises and falls in the flow and watch out for flat spots.

☐ Try to reduce the talk to headings and bullet points.

I never was happy, never could make a good impromptu speech, without several hours to prepare it.

• • •

Mark Twain

CHAPTER 9

Minimise Distractions

• • •

The sobering thing about public speaking is that we could be the most compelling speaker in the world (people may have travelled hundreds of miles to hear us and sold their grandmother's heirloom to pay for the ticket), but if somebody gets up to go to the toilet in the middle of our presentation, half the audience – trust me – will turn to look at them as though they were seeing this phenomenon for the first time in their lives. We've just talked about the necessity of keeping our eyes on our listeners, now we turn to a far harder task: keeping their eyes on *us*.

We may feel this goal shouldn't be difficult at all. After all we're on a stage, in a pulpit, or behind the lectern in an auditorium. But, as we've already seen, a myriad of things can conspire to distract an audience. Without doubt, one of the greatest is the mobile phone. How to deal with this is not easy, and it's not just public speakers who have the problem. There has been a recent spate of theatres banning people who have used their phones during performances, and at least one where a production was stopped because actors became suspicious that someone in the front row was filming it. In another case, an actor was so annoyed to have his lines interrupted by a ringing phone that he grabbed the offending article off the audience member and threw it across the stage.

But in many public speaking contexts, an outright ban on the audience using their phones is not quite so straightforward. People may be using them to make notes, follow a reading or to be contactable by a baby-sitter. And we may well want them to be tweeting about us as we speak. That's all very well, but the problem remains that, unless they are very disciplined, it won't stop them being distracted by emails, text messages, and offers of free holidays in Barbados.

So what should we do? It's not easy, but I think in some contexts it is quite appropriate to ask the audience that, for other people's sake, they at least make sure their phones are on silent. And in some cases, we can even suggest that their phones are switched off or on airplane mode for their *own* sakes (good luck with that one!).

But why is dealing with distractions well so very important? It is because we are trying to protect *the atmosphere.*

Don't break the magic

The relationship between a speaker and the audience has been described as a contract. It occurs in a world in which the usual norms of communication are suspended for a while. When an accomplished public speaker is at work the audience will often forget that they are in a large auditorium; they will feel totally engrossed in an argument, an exposition or a story. If possible, we need to avoid breaking that atmosphere. Unfortunately, a great many things can do this. A mobile phone going off, the wrong PowerPoint slide, or, as we'll see later, poor sound can all change the atmosphere in a moment.

It was 7.00 p.m. on 6th May 2018. The Emirates Stadium was packed to capacity and Arsenal had just beaten Burnley 5–0. But in some ways the game was a sideshow; the real action was around the fact that Arsène Wenger, the Arsenal manager, was leaving the club after over twenty years.

To watch the footage of that event is incredibly moving. As Wenger comes out of the tunnel the crowd goes wild – the standing ovation seems to last forever. And then Wenger moves to the centre of the pitch and begins to address everyone. This is a moment of pure theatre, with a cast of sixty thousand – players, ex-players, directors and, of course, the fans – all privileged to be part of this incredible occasion.

There is no doubt that something very unusual was happening in this 'contract' between speaker and audience, but it wasn't until I had watched the footage dozens of times that it dawned on me what Wenger had achieved in the opening moments of that speech: it was *intimacy*. With more than sixty thousand people in the stadium, that might have seemed an impossible task, but he did it.

He began by wishing his old adversary, Alex Ferguson, the former manager of Manchester United, well; Ferguson was fighting for his life after a brain tumour. Then Wenger went on to thank the fans for 'having me for such a long time. I know this was not easy.' This sounds like a husband thanking his wife for patience on their fiftieth wedding anniversary. And then Wenger said something totally brilliant: 'Above all, I'm like you – I'm an Arsenal fan.' The crowd went wild. 'This isn't a multi-millionaire football manager speaking – this is somebody just like me.' I believe Wenger was being sincere – and it showed. Grown men were rubbing their eyes, visibly moved. Wenger begins to talk about Arsenal's values. This is a magical moment. And then it happens . . . the sound fails.

At first it just stutters, but then there is complete silence as a mic with the name and logo of Arsenal Football Club emblazoned on the side of it packs in completely. Wenger is still speaking, but we can't hear a word. The crowd begin to do a slow hand clap, either in sympathy or frustration. After a couple of seconds, a sound engineer hands Wenger a replacement mic (with no Arsenal logo on the side) and he continues. He does well and manages to recover, but we never did get to hear what Arsenal's values were. A spectacle that involved hundreds of thousands of pounds was spoiled by what may have been a dud battery in a power pack. In that moment, the magic was broken.

Of course, most public speaking is different to Wenger's farewell, save for this: an effective speaker will try to build a bond with the audience. As we speak, they are entering into our arguments, they are catching our passion, and they may even be putting themselves into the stories that we are telling. Part of the task of being an effective speaker is to keep that bond unbroken – to keep the audience's eyes on us, because that eye contact can easily be lost – and in dozens of ways. And it also means that if the chairperson stays on the stage during the talk, they should make every effort to look engrossed in what the speaker is saying and, if necessary, laugh at stories or jokes they've heard many times before. And even if they or others on the platform are making notes, they shouldn't be on their mobile phones – if they are engaged with the speaker it's easier for the audience to concentrate on the speaker too. We need to do everything we can to make sure that the atmosphere is not broken and, if it is, to deal with it as effectively as we possibly can.

Preparation

As we saw when considering our actual delivery, so much of this is in the preparation. We need to do a proper sound check – and not just the main microphone as in Wenger's case, but also the backup. If we need a lectern, we would be wise to check that it is the right height and, preferably, that it is placed to the side of us so that it creates as little a barrier between us and the audience as possible. Perspex is good and sometimes a simple music stand is less intrusive than a lectern that is so huge it looks as though it has been built to withstand the Siege of Mafeking.

Another part of defending that atmosphere is to make sure the doors of the auditorium at the back and sides are closed while we are speaking, and we may want to ask stewards not to move about during the presentation if possible.

As part of the preparation, it's a good idea to have a last check of our appearance. If a zip is undone or we've got spinach in our teeth then good luck with trying to keep the audience's attention on 'Opportunities and Dangers in the Global Village'. And while on the subject of dress, our look should be appropriate: in other words, suitable for the occasion but not so as to draw attention to us personally and cause a distraction from what we are talking about.

In all these things, we are trying to do everything we can to minimise disruption in areas over which we, at least, have some control. But let's take a moment to look at some areas in which we are often not in the driving seat.

People getting out of their seat and walking out

Years ago, when people did this we assumed they were either going to the toilet or that we had offended them. These days, people walk out all the time simply because a call or text message has come through on their mobile.

Whatever the reason, the way to deal with it is the same: don't follow them with your eyes. In fact, try to look in another direction. If you appear entirely engrossed in what you are saying, your audience will be too.

The clatter of tables being cleared

When speaking at a breakfast or dinner, I ask for all the drinks to be served and plates cleared away before I start speaking. This is not being a prima donna; it is born out of years of trying to connect with an audience against the background noise of plates clattering. No doubt this event matters to the organisers, and I want to do as well as I possibly can for them.

I was at a dinner not long ago where one of the main speakers was a literary academic. At the end of his speech, he recited a most moving poem – well, it would have been moving if it hadn't been drowned out by the chinking of cups as coffee was being served. This is not the fault of the waiters or even the catering company. It is the responsibility of the event organiser – and if they forget, remind them.

Air conditioning

Some air conditioning units remind me of the old story of the man who kept banging his head against a wall. When a passer-by asked him why he did it he said, 'It feels so good when I stop.' It's often not until we turn an air-conditioning unit off that we really grasp what a dreadful noise it has been making all along. I've had the privilege of speaking in a variety of churches and auditoriums, and there are very few where it seems that the designers have agonised over the conflicting demands of silence and cool air. To achieve both is not easy and often expensive. Generally, there's little we can do about noisy air-conditioning, but in extreme cases it might be worth considering having it on full blast until you start speaking, then turning it back on in the interval, and so on.

Question time

I hesitate to list this as one of the main distractions as it can often be a valuable part of a presentation – and very important for certain members of the audience. Nevertheless, I have often watched very good talks descend into oblivion because of an ill-considered or ill-handled question time. So I would simply urge you to think very carefully about having questions at the end of your talk. For certain presentations, the chance for the audience to ask questions will be crucial; but in others it can kill a motivational or challenging talk. The last words your audience hears from the presentation are important. If the chairperson asks for questions and there are none, it can destroy the atmosphere. And, perhaps even worse, if the last question is negative or confrontational it can mean that the audience leaves in an agitated state of mind.

Alternatively, and if it's practical, perhaps offer to remain around for a while after your talk to speak to people personally. Another possibility is to have questions at certain intervals during the talk or, if the audience is small, to allow people to gesture if they have a question at any point.

If you do have to allow questions at the end of a talk, make sure that you take back control with some final closing words. And if it's important to send people away with a sense of motivation or challenge, save a story or perhaps a quote to end with.

People who invite you to speak will often say, 'We'd like questions at the end.' Don't agree too quickly. Have the confidence to discuss it with the organiser and consider the options so you ensure the audience has the very best experience.

The above distractions can all break the connection with listeners that we are striving for, but now we come to the mother of all distractors – one so potent that it gets a chapter to itself.

Minimise Distractions

CHECKLIST

☐ Take your role as protector of the atmosphere seriously.

☐ Ask the chairman to request that the audience at least put their phones on silent.

☐ Day of event preparation: sound check; type of lectern and its height; doors of auditorium closed; your appearance; air conditioning.

☐ When speaking at breakfast or dinner, ask for drinks to be served and plates cleared away before you begin your talk.

☐ Consider the options when a question time is requested. Will this give the audience the best experience?

Ninety per cent of how well the talk will go is determined before the speaker steps on the platform.

• • •

Somers White

CHAPTER 10

PowerPoint Pros and Cons

• • •

I have seen speakers use PowerPoint and other visual presentation aids brilliantly – it's as if their oral presentation and the material on the screen is a seamless whole. They are virtuosos of the art – watching them at work is like seeing a concert pianist at the peak of their career: they use PowerPoint to connect and it is powerful, a thing of beauty. For many in the audience, simple headings introducing the different sections of the talk can be very helpful for note-taking and aiding recall. And, of course, for some speakers the material they present means that the visual element is very important. I've often seen extremely moving or challenging video footage used in talks and this only increases connection with the audience.

And I have seen the opposite of that. Watching some speakers use PowerPoint is like watching a butcher attack a piece of meat. They use it to mangle, dismember and, in short, ruin a perfectly good talk.

There seems to be a growing trend away from PowerPoint, perhaps because speakers realise that when we do use it – or indeed any other presentation software – we take an audience's eyes off us and on to something else. We can pay a heavy price for that. We had better be sure it's a price *worth* paying.

Personally, I use PowerPoint very little and just recently I read that many public speakers in the business world have ditched it. It seems that I have managed to become fashionable by the sheer passage of time!

One negative element that causes audiences to tire a bit is 'the next slide' expectation. And, of course, another difficulty is that 'the next slide' inhibits the speaker changing direction even if he or she feels it would help. So, to paraphrase Longfellow's poem about the little girl: 'When it is good, it is very, very good. But when it is bad, it is horrid.' And it tends to be 'horrid' in at least three situations.

First, speakers show a slide that is so text-heavy the audience can hardly see it from the front row. I have heard many speakers say something like, 'Sorry – you probably can't see this from the back.' If you are trying to build a connection with an audience, why would you make a whole section of it feel as if you don't care if they can read the screen or not? It's comparable to an opera singer saying, 'Some of you in the balcony may not be able to hear me when I get to the quieter parts of the piece, so the stewards are going to hand out some printed copies of the lyrics.'

Having said that, PowerPoint works well when, instead of simply listening to the speaker reading a large amount of text, the audience can follow it on the screen. The speaker almost certainly has to lose eye contact to read the passage, but at least the audience is still engaged with the presentation. The only time not to do this is when the reading has some dramatic element, for example, a very moving last line. You will not want to give the game away with the whole thing on the screen.

Second, the PowerPoint distracts because it contains errors – normally spelling – that are off-putting and, at times, hilarious. I've been in church services where the words of a song on a slide have contained the same spelling mistakes for years.

And thirdly, PowerPoint distracts when it simply doesn't work. For example, if it's controlled from the sound desk, it's not uncommon to have a conversation similar to this in front of the audience:

Speaker: 'As our time together comes to an end, I want to show you a quote from Nelson Mandela that changed my life forever.'

[Person controlling the PowerPoint puts up the wrong slide.]

Speaker: 'No, not that one – go back a little.'

[Person controlling the PowerPoint puts up another wrong slide.]

Speaker: 'No, no – back further.'

[Another wrong slide.]

Speaker: 'No – not that far back.'

[Person controlling PowerPoint shouts to the speaker, 'Those are the only ones you gave me.']

Speaker: 'Oh, don't worry. I'll read the quote out . . . "There is no passion to be found playing small – in settling for a life that is . . ."']

['Got it!' shouts the person running the PowerPoint. Correct quote suddenly appears on the screen.]

It would have been better to have ditched the whole PowerPoint presentation the second it threatened not to work because, by now, large sections of the audience have lost the will to live. The speaker tries to recover, but he doesn't notice that three small birds have just flown out of a window in the auditorium: their names are 'Emotion', 'Credibility' and 'Connection'.

We have already talked about the challenges of building a strong sense of connection with an audience. In the next two chapters we consider two elements that, in my experience, many public speakers simply do not pay enough attention to. We could be the finest public speaker in the world, but if we get these two things wrong our talk will be nothing like as effective as we had hoped. Conversely, we may not be the greatest public speaker, but getting these two components right will allow our presentation to be more effective than we had dreamed was possible. So what are they? . . . Sound and seating.

PowerPoint Pros and Cons
CHECKLIST

☐ Every time you show a PowerPoint slide you take the audience's eyes off you. Make sure that is a price worth paying.

☐ If you do use PowerPoint – or any other presentation software – try to configure it in a way that means you will not be totally boxed in if you want to change direction.

☐ Check your presentation for spelling or grammatical errors.

☐ Before you start your talk, make sure that all presentation equipment and software is working properly. If PowerPoint is being controlled remotely, have a run-through with the technician who will be operating it.

Often, people come to a
conclusion about your
presentation by the time
you're on the second slide.
After that, it's often too late
for your bullet points to do
you much good.

• • •

Seth Godin

CHAPTER 11

Sound Matters

• • •

As I write, the Spice Girls are in the middle of their new European Reunion Tour. Attendances will touch almost three-quarters of a million and the total take will be slightly over £62 million. So, after the first two concerts, what is it that is being blogged about and tweeted across the world? Is it the brilliance of Viva Forever, Mama or Wannabe? No. What fans are talking about, journalists writing about, and concert promoters shaking their heads about is – the sound. Fans are complaining they couldn't even understand the group when they were talking to the crowd, let alone when they were singing.

Mark Savage, the BBC Music reporter, asked Robb Allan, one of the industry's leading sound experts, what was going on. The following is the first line of a reply he gave (by the way, this guy has been in the business for a long time, mixing concerts for bands like Massive Attack and Radiohead): 'Sound quality may not have been the top priority for the Spice Girls.'

Allan went on to say that, with a huge pop band, quite often the most important thing is the set – the lights, the video, the choreography – but, 'if we can't put our speakers in the right place because of video screens . . . or the stage, it makes it harder.' And then he said something that should be engraved above the door of every venue in the world where people are trying to convey words using amplification: 'It's an old roadie cliché: "At the end of the day, nobody goes home humming the lights."'

Don't be too hard on Mel B *et al*. The Spice Girls simply join a long line of conference venues, business forums and churches where, for some reason, somebody thought that the sound wasn't the most important thing. Oh, they all believed that speaking was important: they flew prestigious business leaders halfway across the world to share the secrets of their success; they prepared sermon series many months in advance; and they invited politicians to share their vision for a new tomorrow. And the speakers they invited did what they were asked: they explained how a chance encounter in Starbucks in Silicon

Valley changed forever their business model; they taught about the early Church; they explained fiscal policy, GDP trends, and the future for social care. The only problem was that half the audience couldn't hear a word. It is staggering how little attention we often give to the quality of the sound.

Start with the sound

Some years ago, I was invited to attend an event at one of the most prestigious venues in the United Kingdom. The invitation I received was printed on thick white card with gold edging. When I eventually got through security and entered the function room, I was offered white or red wine, champagne or elderflower juice. As I stood sipping my drink, a waiter brought around the most delicious canapés. I glanced around the room. Among the two hundred or so present, I recognised faces from television, the arts world, and several eminent politicians. And then came the time for the main presentation. The invited speaker was an international expert who had been flown in from Seattle. She took the podium – the only thing separating her from the audience being the single microphone on a stand in front of her. She began to speak:

'We used to believe that the greatest threat to mankind would come from a nuclear reactor, but now we know differently. The thing we fear most is . . .' Those at the back of the room never did get to discover what it was that we fear most because the microphone decided to go for a walk. Well, not a walk exactly, but it began to slowly slide downward like the stem of a drooping flower. The nut that was meant to hold it firmly in place in front of the speaker's mouth was loose. We watched, spellbound, as the mic made its slow but determined way towards the floor. The speaker had some notes in one hand and a PowerPoint control in the other, so she did the only thing she felt she could: she bent her knees and for a few seconds tried to follow it down. By any standards it was a gallant effort, but it became apparent very quickly that the mic possessed a greater agility than she did, and finally she pushed the stand to one side and said, 'I think I can manage without the mic.' From that moment on, at least a third of the audience didn't hear a word.

It was nice to get an invitation embossed with gold. The wine and canapés were delicious, and I'm sure the fee and the business-class seat paid to the speaker were worth every penny. But did nobody think to invest in a sound engineer and the hire of some decent equipment for two hours? Somebody should have told them:

'Nobody goes home challenged to change the world by the taste of the canapés.'

Even if you are speaking to twelve kids in a children's club, the sound is important. If possible, find a room that is free from extraneous noise. Don't simply accept the fact that a teenage band are practising next door and there's nothing that can be done about it. The things you are sharing with those kids are life-changing. They need to hear them. Sound matters.

If you are designing any venue in which amplified speech is important, start with the sound. Don't have an air conditioning system that drowns out almost every word from the platform the second it's turned on. Don't have great coffee and second-rate amplification speakers. And don't have well-meaning volunteers manning the sound desk who don't understand it properly. Instead, spend time training those who manage the sound and, if it's feasible, be prepared to work with a small number who really know how to use the equipment – including microphones. Just last month I listened to a great talk, but it was spoiled because the hand-held mic kept 'popping'. If only somebody had taken a few moments to show the speaker the best place to have held it (about six inches from his mouth).

The area where I live is full of old chapels – many built during the great religious revivals of the late nineteenth and early twentieth centuries. None of them were constructed with electronic amplification, but you can speak from the pulpit in almost all of them and be heard in every corner of the building. Those who built these chapels were often not wealthy, and the fabric is frequently evidence of that, but they put money and consideration into the sound – the placing of the pulpit, the arrangement of the seating (often a horseshoe shape), and the height of the ceilings – to ensure that people could hear. I have spoken at conferences in fancy hotels on Park Lane, London, that could have learnt a thing or two from the old chapel builders.

As public speakers today, the sound should matter to us too. Having the best sound possible will enhance the audience's reaction to what we say. If we are speaking week by week in the same church, we can use whatever influence we have to get the best sound possible within that church's budget. But if we travel to different speaking venues, we don't have that level of control; we just have to use whatever equipment and manpower it has. However, we are not completely powerless.

Mics and sound checks

First of all, before you turn up to speak, ask the organisers what kind of microphones are available. If you like to have both hands free, for example, a hand-held mic is not going to be ideal for you; you'll be more comfortable with a lapel, head or stand mic. And, depending on the type of mic we will use, what we wear can sometimes be important. If it's a lapel mic, do we have a top or collar we can attach it to? And if the mic has a battery pack, it's important to wear something that can house it – I'm told that finding a home for that contraption when the speaker is wearing a dress is not the easiest task!

I like to get to a venue early enough to do a sound check. Often somebody will say to me, 'Oh, we've checked it – it's fine.' But my voice is not their voice – and anyway it won't do me any harm to have a few moments using that equipment and hearing for myself how it sounds. Of course, we'll need to arrive early enough to do that, preferably before the audience is seated. But even if a few early birds are in the room, it's still worth doing. I normally say something like, 'I'm going to do a quick sound check – I won't be long', so they don't think the event has started and they are the only ones there!

And I would encourage you to do a proper sound check. Don't just stand on the stage tapping the end of the mic and saying, 'Testing, testing – one, two, three!' We need to speak long enough for the sound engineer to have time to adjust the levels. (I was once at an event where the guy working the sound was trying to find the right level as the solo soprano on stage was actually singing.) But it can be embarrassing doing a sound check if you're not sure what to say, and if there are people in the room, you don't want to use any of your material – you'll want to save that. So, I have a poem and a piece of prose that I use alternately. One is Wordsworth's poem about daffodils. If you ever come to hear me speak and get there early, you may see me on stage in front of an empty auditorium spouting, 'I wandered lonely as a cloud.' And as I am doing that sound check I ask, if possible, for team members or volunteers to walk to different parts of the room to check if the sound is good in each location.

Let me mention two final things on the subject of sound. When using a radio mic, always ask the sound engineer if the batteries are new. There's nothing worse than being halfway through a talk and the power failing. And lastly, have a backup mic available – probably hand-held – and put it in a place where you can grab it quickly if your main mic fails.

Sound matters. After all, nobody ever goes home humming the lights.

Sound Matters
CHECKLIST

☐ Start with the sound. If people can't hear, everything else, however good, is worthless.

☐ Prioritise doing a proper sound check.

☐ When using a radio mic, always ask the sound engineer if the batteries are new, and have a backup mic available if your main mic fails.

I do not object to people looking at their watches when I am speaking. But I do strongly object when they start shaking them to make sure they are still going.

• • •

Lord Birkett

CHAPTER 12

Optimise the Seating

• • •

When I was a child, my parents didn't go to church but they sent me to the Sunday school in the little chapel on the corner of our street. It was there that I met one of the greats in the area of public speaking: Miss Williams. It is true that our Sunday school teacher never did get to address audiences of more than about fifteen in number, but most public speakers who think themselves brilliant wouldn't have a chance of keeping the attention of a group of eight-year-olds. It is only now, as I look back, that I realise how skilled she was.

First, Miss Williams was a brilliant raconteur – we loved her stories. Second, she was an aficionado of the classic rhetorical devices – pitch, pause and pace. Her voice would rise and fall with the drama of David and Goliath's story: she would slow down as David came face to face with the giant, speed up as the young shepherd boy rushed toward the prostrate Goliath and stood over him, and finally, she would pause and say, 'Boys and girls, we all have giants to fight – don't be scared of them.'

But it's only very recently, as I've spent time thinking about the ideal seating layout for connecting with an audience, that I've realised why Miss Williams always went into the little room we used for our classroom about five minutes before we kids trooped out of the main church service: she understood the importance of getting the seating right. The chairs were always in a horseshoe shape with her chair in the centre and there were always exactly the right number – there were never any empty ones. One Sunday when it seemed that chickenpox had practically wiped out our primary school, she put out just six chairs. Miss Williams understood that when it comes to connection, the way you set out the chairs matters. I don't care whether you are running a business event in a hotel or a church service – most of us could learn a thing or two from my old Sunday school teacher.

Pay attention to layout

Often there is not much you can do as a speaker about the layout of the room – in many auditoriums or churches the seating is fixed – but if there is flexible seating, think carefully about the arrangement of the chairs. Anything you can do to optimise the seating will make a massive difference to an audience's experience – it affects both atmosphere and connection. If you have a full house, the seating will probably be fine as it is, but if numbers are low, it's vital to think carefully about layout. Imagine that you are disappointed with the numbers coming in and are expecting only seventy-five people in a 400-seater auditorium. The problems of connecting with so few people in a large space are great enough without allowing the delegates to scatter themselves all over the venue.

In this scenario, arrange just one hundred chairs in a tight horseshoe shape in front of the stage (as long as you are prepared to help put them back afterwards!). The horseshoe shape increases a sense of intimacy and makes eye contact easier. If possible, put some screens behind the back row (pull-up banners will do fine for this). You are trying to create as intimate a setting as possible. Then move the lectern from the stage or pulpit to the floor in front of the chairs to decrease the distance between yourself and the audience. The principle is exactly the same if you have 500 people turn up in a 1,000-seater auditorium – except that you can't move the lectern to the floor because the people at the back simply won't see you.

And no matter how many people are attending, always try to fill the front row. At Care for the Family events we put delicious chocolates on the front seats and ask the stewards to nudge people towards them!

Try not to have a centre aisle. Why would you want to give a talk looking straight out at thin air? The area in front of the lectern is the prime space in which to achieve audience connection, which you hope will spread throughout the auditorium. Cinemas and theatres do not have centre aisles for this very reason.

One last point on the matter of numbers who attend: some years ago, I was on a speaking tour overseas and the numbers at the events were good except for one where very few tickets had been sold. When I asked the organisers if they were worried, they gave me the same answer I've heard all over the world: 'Oh, no. People in Sydney/Aberdeen/Chiswick/Barbados/Guatemala/Upper Wapping always book at the last minute.' The auditorium could seat up to fifteen hundred, so I asked, 'How many chairs are you going to put out?' They said, 'Six hundred.' I said, 'Please – trust me – put out 200 chairs and let's make the place look as full as we can. People will have a better experience.' They resisted and eventually we did the deal at 400 chairs. When I got to the venue my face fell. Never mind 400 chairs – it looked to me as though they'd hired in chairs from every auditorium in the country – the placed was stuffed with seats. The event began at 7.00 p.m. By 6.50 p.m. there were fifty people who looked bemused at the incredible choice of places available. By the time we began, that number had somehow dribbled up to 120.

I spoke during the first half and in the interval a young man came up to me. He said, 'You speak all over the world, don't you?' I replied, 'Yes, I do.'

'And you often speak to large audiences, don't you?' I gave an embarrassed cough and nodded. He said, 'I found tonight impressive. You have spoken to us as though there were thousands here.' I was encouraged that he'd noticed a principle I have practised all my speaking life: if you believe you have something worth saying, then try with all your might to get as many people as possible to come and hear it. But when the event begins and you stand up to speak, forget about how many have actually showed up and give it all you've got.

Optimise the Seating
CHECKLIST

☐ Create as intimate a setting as possible.

☐ Always try to fill the front row.

☐ Try not to have a centre aisle.

☐ Aim to have as few empty chairs as possible. If numbers are lower than the available seating, close off parts of the auditorium, using screens if necessary.

Make sure you have
finished speaking before
your audience has finished
listening.

• • •

Dorothy Sarnoff

CHAPTER 13

Learn to Handle Your Critics

• • •

The world of public speaking has many challenges – and we have considered some of them – preparation, delivery, dealing with distractions, and getting the sound and seating right to list just a few. But now we come to one of the greatest challenges of all: dealing with our critics.

The auditorium is empty, the stewards are tidying up the debris scattered between the seats, and the guys at the sound desk are packing away the microphones. You are a public speaker and your presentation is finished: this is your most vulnerable moment.

It is true that several people came up to you at the end of your talk and were very encouraging, but you cannot get the comment of the man who was so cross with you out of your mind. And if you are like most of us, you may never get it out of your mind. But somehow, as you develop as a public speaker, you must not be defined solely by what people say to you or write to you after your talk. I have often driven home foolishly elated or needlessly low after a speaking event, but with the benefit of the years I have come to believe something that helps me get a little perspective: *most of my triumphs were not as great as I first thought, and most of my disasters not so bad after all.*

If people are kind and wise, they will leave any negative comments for a day or two for it is almost as if our souls are laid bare when we speak. I don't want to be a cynical public speaker, I don't want to 'get used to it', and I know that sometimes I must leave a little of my blood behind on the floor: just don't rub my nose in it straightaway.

Anyway, I have long believed that our critics, not just in public speaking but in life generally, are split into two categories. The first kind are on our side. What they say may hurt a little, but they say it for our good. The Bible says, 'Faithful are the wounds of a friend.' Early on in my speaking career a good friend gave me two pieces of advice. He said first: 'If somebody asks you to speak for thirty minutes, speak for twenty-five. It's rude to speak too long. People will say to you, "Oh,

I could have listened to you all day", but they won't mean it.' Second, he said, 'Stop saying that silly thing at the end of your talks.'

'What silly thing?' I asked.

He said, 'You keep saying, "Oh, I wish we had time to go into this in more detail." Don't do that because people feel cheated – they wonder what they've missed. And if the chairperson said, "Well, actually Rob, we do have another thirty minutes free", you wouldn't have a clue what to talk about.' Ah – faithful are the wounds of a friend.

That same friend went on to mentor me in public speaking for a number of years. He'd often sit at the back of my presentations making copious notes and suggestions. Thankfully, as the years went by, the notes grew shorter. I am deeply grateful to him.

Evaluation makes perfect

Our critics are important. We often say, 'practice makes perfect', but I think it is more accurate to say, 'practice with *evaluation* makes perfect'. If you practise your bad golf swing every day for a year, in twelve months' time you will have an even more effective *bad* swing. As public speakers, we are fortunate if we can find a 'critical friend', somebody to help us practise with evaluation. And, of course, we can do that job ourselves – we can be our own critic. I often hear speakers say, 'I never listen to myself or watch film footage of my talks – I find it too embarrassing!' But, if we can do it, it's a great way to assess what worked and what didn't. And it can help us spot those little idiosyncrasies that even our best friend isn't courageous enough to tell us about.

But I said there are two categories of critic, and the second kind is not on your side. They do not criticise to build you up – to help you get better at whatever you are doing; they do so to bring you down. In the public-speaking arena they will tell you that your talks are too long or too short, too shallow or too deep; that you use too many stories or are too academic. And although you will try to please them, you never will. I was once with a colleague who had just come off stage having spoken brilliantly to four thousand people. As we made our way towards the exit a man approached him and said, 'I teach people about public speaking – I think I can help you.' I won't tell you what I wanted to say, but it had to do with teaching manners and that I think *I* could have helped *him*. (By the way, if anything in this book has helped you at all, don't be so enthusiastic about it that you give it as a gift to someone straight after their talk!)

So there it is: two kinds of critic – one on our side, one not. We ought, therefore, to be able to accept the criticism of one and ignore the other. If only it were so simple! As much as I hate to admit it, I have come to believe that there is often a grain of truth even in the criticism of those who don't have our best interests at heart. For that reason, it is wise not to dismiss it completely. Don't respond immediately but take a little time a few days later to assess whether any of it is justified.

On the first page of this book I said that one characteristic of the most effective communicators is that they are teachable. And to be teachable we have to listen to our critics – and occasionally both kinds!

Ouch!

Learn to Handle Your Critics
CHECKLIST

☐ Know your critics. There are two kinds: one is on your side, they criticise to build you up; the other criticises to bring you down.

☐ There may be some truth in what the latter group say to you. Take a moment to consider it, but don't spend your life trying to please them.

☐ Remember that most of your triumphs were probably not as great as you first thought, and most of your disasters were probably not so bad after all.

You can't let praise or criticism get to you. It's a weakness to get caught up in either one.

• • •

John Wooden

CHAPTER 14

The Music, a Little Humility and the Hardest Task of All – Ending!

• • •

We are nearly done. I have shared with you some lessons learnt from a lifetime of public speaking – more than a few of them gleaned the hard way! I passionately believe that any one of these could make a difference for good in your presentations. But as we draw to a close, I would like to take a moment to consider something that, I confess, is a little out of the box. I have heard people talk about the 'science' of public speaking almost as if the elements of a good talk were like a list of chemical ingredients. And I have heard others talk about the 'art' of public speaking. But, as I end, I want to suggest that there is sometimes a mysterious third element that is not easy to categorise. Allow me to explain.

Lord Soper was a Methodist minister. He died in 1995 but throughout his life and well into his nineties he preached at London's centres of free speech – Tower Hill and, from 1942, Speaker's Corner in Hyde Park. He was often referred to as 'Dr Soapbox' in honour of the make-shift podium he used to stand on. One day a heckler interrupted him and yelled, 'Eh – Soper! Where's the soul in the body?' He replied, 'Where the music is in the organ.' It was a brilliant answer. You can take the organ apart – examine the keys, the pumps, the pedals and the pipes – but you will never find the music.

Of course, techniques are important but, above all, the most important thing for a speaker to have is 'the music'. You may be able to construct a flawless speech with the use of ethos, logos, and pathos – but the music can still elude you. Your talk can be long, short or in-between, and you can get the seating right, the sound right, and gaze into people's eyes forever – but you can still miss it. I find it strangely reassuring that God can sometimes decide to take somebody who breaks all the rules of communication, yet gift them with – the music.

Remembering that simple fact both encourages and humbles me. I don't know what arena you speak in – perhaps business, education or in the faith community. In my time, I have spoken in all three, but I have learnt, particularly in the last one, that a little humility is not a bad thing.

Some time ago, I was speaking in a church on a Sunday morning and my topic was money and debt. I held forth on that subject for thirty minutes or so, and when I finished speaking I took my seat next to Dianne. Most public speakers are a bit more insecure than we let on, and I was anxious to get her opinion on how the talk had gone. I whispered in her ear, 'How was it?' She replied, 'I'm so sorry, but I can't tell you. I couldn't concentrate – I've been laughing too much.' My whispers increased in volume, 'What do you mean you were laughing too much? I've been talking about debt – people's homes are at risk!' She whispered back, 'You've got odd shoes on.'

I looked down and I did indeed have odd shoes on. Moreover, I didn't recognise the shoe on my left foot. I gazed down at it and it was as if it gazed back up at me, nonchalantly. It was black like the one on my right foot, but it was obviously different – it had a large toecap that looked as if it could withstand a jackhammer. And that's when I realised what had happened. My son is a firefighter and the previous evening he'd come around to stay the night and we'd both kicked off our shoes while watching Match of the Day. That morning, I'd been in a rush getting ready and I'd put one of his boots on by mistake. (And managed to ignore my own 'check your appearance' advice.)

When things like that happen, you hope that people haven't noticed. No such luck. When the service was over nobody commented on how brilliant my talk was. No – they wanted to talk about my shoes. One person said, 'It must be difficult dressing in the dark.' I don't recommend errors in dress code, but having a sense of our own frailty is not a bad thing. As a public speaker and even in life generally, I am sometimes safer when I've got odd shoes on: it stops me taking myself too seriously.

Our time together is almost over and in my mind's eye I am imagining you not as a reader but as a delegate at a conference where I am speaking. You are sitting in seat B6 in the balcony and during my presentation I have been doing my best to keep connection with that section of the audience – at least once or twice, our eyes have met. But now there is only a minute to go and I must do that hardest thing of all: end.

There comes a time in every talk when we simply have to stop speaking and get off that podium. But as any experienced public speaker knows, this is often not as easy as it appears. Two quite different emotions can thwart us in that task: pride and fear. First, pride: we are having such a good time that we assume the audience are too. In my experience, they are rarely having *that* good a time! Have the grace to stop. Second, it may be fear that keeps us from finishing: we feel we have done badly and want to see if we can put it right. Don't make it worse: just end. I have heard so many talks that would have been brilliant if they'd finished ten minutes earlier.

But it can be hard to bring a presentation to a conclusion and, sometimes, it's helpful to have something to use in case you get stuck. One way is briefly to mention some of the things you've already covered and then give a sentence or two to bring it all together. And so, I look up to seat B6 and begin my conclusion:

We've covered a lot of material in *The Heart of Communication*. We've looked at the elements of persuasion: ethos, logos and pathos. We've considered how best to build a strong relationship with an audience and tried to remember that nobody goes home humming the lights. We've talked about keeping the audience's eyes on us and our eyes on them, the power of silence, and a whole lot more. When we began, I said that I wanted you to find one thing that would make a difference in your own public speaking. I hope, with all my heart, that you have done that. But just in case you haven't yet found that one thing, perhaps this final thought could be it: *imagine that this is your last talk.*

Once in a while, particularly if I am a little tired or even discouraged, I will try to do this. And when

I do, I find that it often fills me with fresh energy and encouragement to climb the steps to a podium somewhere and begin, yet again, 'Ladies and gentlemen, it's good to be with you today . . .'

I wish you well in your public speaking. I hope that some of the ideas I have shared will help you in the vital task of not just communicating but *connecting*. And I pray that both you and I may earn what I consider to be one of the highest accolades possible for anybody who seeks to harness the power of words. It was a description given of the greatest communicator who ever lived:

'The common people heard him gladly.'

Also by Rob Parsons

• • •

Bringing Home the Prodigals

Getting Your Kids Through Church Without Them
  Ending Up Hating God

Let Me Tell You a Story

Loving Against the Odds

The Heart of Success

The Money Secret

The Sixty Minute Family

The Sixty Minute Father

The Sixty Minute Grandparent

The Sixty Minute Marriage

The Sixty Minute Mother Talks to Rob Parsons

The Sixty Second Father

The Sixty Second Marriage
The Sixty Second Mother
The Sixty Second Family
The Sixty Second Grandparent
Teenagers! What Every Parent Has to Know
The Wisdom House
What They Didn't Teach Me in Sunday School

Archie and the Amazing Four-Poster Bed

By Rob Parsons and Katharine Hill
The Really, Really Busy Person's Book on Parenting
The Really, Really Busy Person's Book on Marriage

By Rob Parsons and Katie Clarke
The Sixty Minute Debtbuster

By Rob Parsons and Lloyd Parsons
What Every Kid Wished Their Parents Knew . . . and
     Vice Versa

By Rob Parsons and Fiona Castle
Family Matters

Read more about the power of stories

• • •

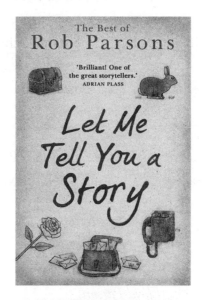

LET ME TELL YOU A STORY

ROB PARSONS

9781473670969

Let Me Tell You a Story brings together some of the very best stories from Rob's career. He shares heartwarming and challenging tales that make up a compendium of insights on faith and family, love and loss, money and priorities, dreams and goals.

Read more about connecting with an audience

• • •

THE WISDOM HOUSE
ROB PARSONS

9781444745672

In my mind's eye, I see my grandchildren sinking into that chair in the years to come. There are so many things I want to share with them — life-changing things I have learned myself, and gleaned from those far wiser than I.

Read more about success

...

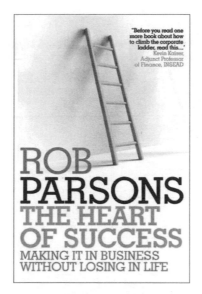

THE HEART OF SUCCESS

ROB PARSONS

9780340995624

'Before you read one more book about how to climb the corporate ladder, read this: it will help you make sure the ladder is leaning against the right wall.' *Kevin Kaiser, Adjunct Professor of Finance, INSTEAD*